The Hutchinson's Guide

to

Developing Effective Mentoring Skills

Transform Self-Limiting Behaviours.

Eileen Hutchinson

The Hutchinson's Guide to Developing Effective Mentoring Skills

Eileen Hutchinson

The Hutchinson's Guide to Developing Effective Mentoring Skills

Table of Contents

1 – 1 - Introduction..1

1 – 2 - The rewards of mentoring 10

1 – 3 - The overlap of coaching and mentoring..11

1 – 4 - The background to mentoring..14

1 – 5 - The principal features of an effective mentor..16

2 – 0 - Barriers to effective mentoring and how to overcome them...................................22

2 – 1 - Defining the characteristics of effective Mentoring...26

2 – 2 - Mentoring models...28

2 – 3 - Mentoring compared to other developmental styles..38

2 – 4 - Understand how to use different questioning and listening techniques....................39

2 – 5 - Principal features of giving feedback and developing trust......................................41

3 – 0 - How to organise mentoring activities..43

3 – 1 - Mentoring records..45

3 – 2 - Practical application of developing mentoring skills...46

3 – 3 - The matching process...47

3 – 4 - The role of supervision in mentoring...48

3 – 5 - Ending the mentoring relationship...50

4 – 0 – The psychology of mentoring..52

4 – 1 - Case studies and templates...54

4 – 1 - References..69

Copyright

All copyright and other intellectual property rights in these materials are owned by the author Eileen Hutchinson. Copying, adaptation or other use of all or any part of these materials without the express written permission of Eileen Hutchinson is strictly prohibited. No part of this publication may be reproduced, stored in a retrieval system or transmitted in any form or by any means (electronic, mechanical, photocopying, recording or otherwise) without the prior written permission of the publisher. Permission may be sought directly from Eileen Hutchinson at www.eileenhutchinson.com

Notice

Every possible effort has been made to ensure that the information contained in this workbook is accurate at the time of being published. No responsibility is assumed by the publisher for any injury and/or damage to persons or property as a matter of products liability, negligence or otherwise, or from any use or operation of any methods, products, instructions or ideas contained in the material herein.

© 2020 Eileen Hutchinson. All rights reserved.

The Hutchinson's Guide is an imprint of Eileen Hutchinson

United Kingdom

Second Edition Version 0.2 22 August 2022

Publisher LULU - ISBN 9781716683640

Acknowledgments

This workbook would not have been completed without the mentoring and support I have received from others, namely working with the management teams at North Hertfordshire College, Hertfordshire Probation Services, Luton and Bedfordshire Chamber of Commerce, The Prince's Trust, TCHC Group, and all the individuals I have had the pleasure to mentor, coach and train. To you all, I want to say, "Thank You"!

I would like to thank Peter Hutchinson, for the unwavering years of support. Peter has proven to be one of the best friends any woman could wish for. My daughter, Emma Hutchinson, for her love and continuous support and my adorable niece, Olivia Pettit, who brings joy, fun and laughter to my life.

Thank you to Carol Godfrey for the hours of editing and helping me to create this workbook. To my long-time friend and mentor Brenda Godden, who has helped me to shine a light on interpersonal awareness. Thank you to you, the reader, and I hope you find the workbook helpful when developing your mentoring skills.

"A mentor empowers a person to see a possible future and believe it can be obtained."
—Shawn Hitchcock

Workbook and programme

This workbook will give you the opportunity to learn and practise new skills and techniques to improve your performance as a mentor. The programme consists of several modules covering different aspects of mentoring with learning tools, techniques and exercises for you to practise.

Whilst the overall objective of this workbook is to facilitate your professional development, the workbook aims to provide you with a balanced viewpoint and understanding through the underpinning and thought-provoking exploration of mentoring. I draw on others' research, acknowledging and referencing their work; I provide materials and findings drawn from my individual research and teachings tools.

Accreditation options

The materials from this workbook may be used to support you on an accredited programme under an agreement between my training company EH Coaching Academy Ltd, an Institute for work-based learning. Specifically, I am able to offer you accreditation options through my Academy - the website can be viewed at www.ehcoachingacademy.com, and we hold centre status from ILM www.i-l-m.com.

Completing the modules can lead you to successfully apply for the ILM Level 2 qualification in Effective Mentoring with EH Coaching Academy. You can use this module towards Levels 3 or 5 in "Effective Coaching and Mentoring". For further information please visit our website. This may also be used as a route to developing leadership and management capabilities. If you follow this accredited route, then the modules are provided alongside educational support and assessment from qualified educational tutors.

Therefore, this workbook is aligned with ILM's accreditation routes, as a recognised programme which includes assessments. The materials in this workbook are cross-referenced with the ILM national standards linked to the "Qualification and Credit Framework" and may be used in conjunction with the following programmes:

ILM Level 2 Award in Effective Mentoring - this Award holds 5 credits and will give you all the skills and knowledge to mentor successfully. The workbook links directly to the Level 2 Award.

The ILM Level 3 Certificate in Effective Coaching is used for coaching in the workplace and team development; it focuses on the skills and knowledge required to coach team members effectively in the workplace and develop their performance. For individuals looking to develop their careers as workplace coaches the ILM Level 3 Certificate in Effective Coaching is an ideal progression route.

The ILM Level 5 Certificate or Diploma in Effective Coaching and Mentoring is ideal if you are a manager with significant responsibility for coaching and mentoring as part of your day-to-day role. It will also support you if you are planning to move into a development role in your organisation or start a career as a freelance coach and mentor. You can use the workbook for the level five criteria as it contains relevant information linked to the course requirements.

If you would like to consider gaining the qualification effective mentoring or coaching, then please contact us via our websites link www.ehcoachingacademy.com www.eileenhutchinson.com

"We're here for a reason. I believe a bit of the reason is to throw little torches out to lead people through the dark." — Whoopi Goldberg

About this workbook

This workbook aims to support you in developing the skills, knowledge and experience necessary to perform well within any mentoring role, whether at work, as a freelancer mentor or community project worker. The exercises and materials will help you understand the role of a mentor, are self-directed and have been designed to strengthen your knowledge and support your development. You should complete the activities in all the sections as you progress through the chapters.

This workbook and programme will help you provide employees or mentees with the tools they need to ensure they have the right level of understanding to undertake the role of a mentor. By studying and practising the skills, techniques and tools used in the mentoring role, you will improve performance and move towards becoming an accredited mentor. The accreditation programme consists of interactive training exercises and assessments via our E-learning classroom.

You will gain additional benefits and outcomes from reviewing, answering the questions, and completing the exercises, and you will be guided through this process step by step.

The exercises will help you to:
- Develop practical skills in mentoring.
- Develop the ability to make informed choices on the mentoring approaches you want to use in your mentoring practice, including theories and mentoring models.
- Understand the importance of work-based or life issues to facilitate the mentoring process without bias, and to enable you to understand your own limitations.

You may already be in a mentoring relationship, or you may be new to the whole concept of mentoring. Whichever one is true for you, be assured that you will be presented with all the information you require to develop your skills as an effective mentor.

This workbook openly explores the knowledge, experience and understanding required to develop practical mentoring skills with a focus on business and interpersonal development. I have found a mentoring culture enables organisations to address fundamental challenges in breaking down barriers and drive lasting change by initiating mentoring as part of their continuous professional development.

Mentoring can assist you in achieving your goals and objectives by looking at pressing and long-term goals, including those that stretch you. A mentoring culture develops responsive thinking and creativity and regularly deals with the broader background of your personal life.

Once you have read all the material provided, you will be ready to progress within the mentoring role and offer mentoring sessions to a mentee. Remember, you are always encouraged to reflect on all the mentoring sessions you engage in. I encourage you to use the experience as a basis for your reflective practice, which is a process of self-analysis where you reflect on your thoughts, feelings and actions.

You should gain insight from the mentoring relationships you develop to support your mentoring skills further. You can make use of the planning and reflective exercises presented throughout, giving you practical tools and techniques to use in your mentoring practice or download them for free from our website www.ehcoachingacademy.com

"Self-awareness and self-love move you towards self-acceptance."
—*Eileen Hutchinson*

Who is this book for?

This book will support you in developing effective mentoring skills and will aid you in the completion of the ILM Award in Effective Mentoring. The aims are to equip individuals, team leaders and aspiring first-time managers with the skills and knowledge to understand and undertake effective mentoring to aid their own personal development.

Results and benefits for you or your team members:
- Reflect on your own performance
- Plan for effective mentoring sessions
- Learn essential listening and questioning techniques
- Understand how to organise mentoring activities
- Utilise mentoring skills to reflect on your own performance
- Develop an understanding of the role and nature of mentoring
- Define the goals, progress and actions needed for mentoring

Impact for your employer, business, or clients:
- Give team leaders and aspiring first-time managers the skills they need to progress and develop
- Develop a mentoring culture in your organisation by introducing essential mentoring skills and techniques
- Define the goals, progress and actions needed to improve your performance by completing the CPD activity planner

Focus on the skills you need

The exercises presented are practical and will give you a full understanding of mentoring within the workplace, school, charity, or as a project worker or volunteer.

There are two mandatory units in the ILM Award. Unit 1 Understanding Mentoring - helps learners develop an understanding of the role and nature of mentoring, while unit 2 Developing Mentoring Skills - enables learners to undertake mentoring to reflect on their performance and identify areas for improvement.

EH packages – For those of you who wish to take the accreditation route - You will receive:
1. Access to E-learning classroom, online assessment, and support throughout the course.
2. Online mentoring and support via phone or video conferencing with your tutor, who will support you every step of the way.
3. CPD and access to a pool of coaches, mentors, and a study group.
4. Opportunity to join our bimonthly book club

ILM studying membership

You will receive free studying membership for the duration of your studies. All learners currently studying for an ILM qualification enjoy the benefits of membership completely free during the training period. A key benefit for learners is access to ILM's learning and development portal. It provides over 400 digital learning resources, developed by leading experts, covering essential leadership and management topics which are all mapped to ILM qualifications.

"In learning you will teach, and in teaching you will learn."
— Phil Collins

Qualification assessment
The qualification consists of two units: one Knowledge-based and one skills-based, which are both assessed internally and subject to internal and external verification.

Units - 8584-200 Understanding mentoring - Assignment tasks
You are about to become a mentor and want to ensure you are thoroughly prepared for the task. In order to do this, you will need to find out more about best practice for the mentoring role. Provide an answer for all the following tasks:

Task 1 - In this task, before you begin your new work, you are finding out more about what the mentor does, the benefits and any potential barriers.
- 1-1 Considering your new mentoring role in supporting individuals, describe the essential parts of the work and the main activities of an effective mentor.
- 1-2 Outline the main benefits of the mentoring you are about to undertake by describing at least three situations where the mentoring will add value. Describe how mentoring can benefit those being mentored in a range of situations.
- 1-3 There are likely to be potential barriers which will affect the success of your mentoring. Outline two or more and explain why they are each a potential barrier.
- 1-4 Provide an explanation of how to overcome each of the potential barriers to effective mentoring that you have identified.

Task 2 - In this task, you are now considering how best to prepare yourself for practical mentoring. The learning outcome will enable you to understand what makes a mentor effective in their role.
- 2-1 Consider the key skills you need to be effective in your role as a mentor. Present a list of these skills in a table which gives essential information about those skills.
- 2-2 Select a model or process that you are planning to follow with an individual in your mentoring sessions and describe how it will work in your organisation or situation.
- 2-3 Explain how you are going to use your knowledge of questioning and listening techniques effectively in mentoring individuals, and how they will support individuals being mentored.
- 2-4 Part of your role will be to give feedback to individuals - describe how you will do this in an effective way.
- 2-5 It will take time to develop trust with individuals in mentoring situations. Describe what can be done to achieve this.

Task 3 - In this task, you are making sure that you are fully prepared for the mentoring role and you will select relevant documents to complete.
- 3-1 Explain your method for planning effective mentoring sessions and how you will plan to use any forms or templates as evidence.
- 3-2 Select at least two goals that would be agreed between you and the individual you are mentoring and describe what you would consider for the goals to become effective.
- 3-3 Give reasons for the selection of records that the mentor is required to keep, identifying examples and explaining the main considerations in keeping those records.

"Effective mentoring empowers communities, institutes and businesses to address fundamental challenges by investing in the interpersonal development of employees and volunteers."
—Eileen Hutchinson

1-1 Introduction to effective mentoring.

Like many others who got into mentoring in the early days, mentoring found me, quite a few years ago, I was seconded to probation services, offering ETE (Education Training and Employment Advice). It soon became apparent to my line managers at North Herts College and Probation Services that the work I was doing was having an incredible impact on the lives of individuals in the criminal justice system. The effect enabled people to make significant changes in their lives, supporting them to move away from a life of crime and become honest citizens within our communities.

The work I was doing was recorded and filmed by Probation Services in Hertfordshire and shown nationally at conferences throughout the UK. My employers at North Herts College were delighted by the attention we were receiving, which reached the Head of the criminal justice system within the UK Government. This led to the Government arranging to visit our programme accompanied by our local MP, Barbara Follett. The visit congratulated us on the success we had achieved by helping ex-offenders turn their lives around. I then began to get calls from other probation services, asking if I could offer work shadowing to their ETE advisors, and this is when my journey of providing mentoring to others commenced.

This book contains the materials I would have liked to have had at my disposal during that time. Throughout that period, I was making new inroads into working with individuals who were seeking to change their behaviours. I did not know of anyone else who was doing what I was doing but, unknown to me; numerous other forerunners were also discovering their mentoring craft.

As I started to mentor others in the way I worked, I did not appreciate the innate abilities I was conveying. I was somewhat perplexed by the attention I received as all I was doing, I thought, was common sense. However, I now understand that my deep compassion for supporting people, who I felt were less fortunate in life, was at the very heart of my work. I was engaging with others on an equal footing, i.e. I was not judging them for what they had done. I was not acting in an authoritarian way, but I showed the courage of daring to be at one with people who needed to feel that someone believed in them.

I have developed this workbook with several different audiences in mind, and with one common theme, the desire to understand how mentoring works. Writing this book has enabled me to talk about mentoring from many different perspectives, and from the numerous hours of mentoring and teaching others to achieve a mentoring or coaching qualification. With this in mind, my intention is to share with you the magic ingredients that define mentoring relationships.

Together, the chapters, reviews and tools explore how and why mentoring can play a role in promoting excellent interpersonal development. I hope this workbook becomes part of your vocational learning or CPD, which will broaden your understanding of mentoring delivery and increase your enthusiasm for additional mentoring courses or qualifications.

Today I work as a qualified business mentor, trainer, supervisor, SFEDI advisor and assessor. My work includes working on various business enterprises throughout the UK and initiating business mentoring training and workforce development with partners to deliver government contracts. I was part of a team who assessed 'Business Link Advisors' in East Anglia, working with the Luton and Bedfordshire Chamber of Commerce, and I am proud to have been a business mentor with The Prince's Trust.

"Do things at your own pace as life is not a race."
—*Eileen Hutchinson*

Personal goals

I open this section by asking you to consider the ILM Award objectives and your personal goals for completing this workbook or course. In the box below, note the outcomes you would like to achieve in terms of knowledge, skills or interpersonal awareness. This activity will also help you structure your continuous personal development plan (CPD), a requirement for anyone practising as a mentor.

---

1) Knowledge

2) Skills

3) Interpersonal awareness

4) Other development needs

"I've learned a lot from mentors who were instrumental in shaping me, and I want to share what I've learned." — Herbie Hancock

---

1-2 The rewards of mentoring

I understand for most employees; mentoring may not be part of your daily work. Still, I wonder if you know that many companies that have implemented a mentoring scheme have developed a successful employee engagement strategy. Mentoring within the workplace is now recognised as a rewarding experience in developing employees by equipping them with the mentoring skills to impact the overall business success.

My experience and mentoring knowledge are gained from creating and implementing mentoring schemes within the business and voluntary sector and research with North Hertfordshire University, leading to the development of the successful peer-to-peer mentoring programme, which is now being delivered by Mind within the UK. I have included reflections from developing that programme at the end of the book, alongside additional resources you may find helpful when growing your mentoring skills.

My work also extended to creating an innovative mentoring programme for ex-offenders, working alongside SOVA and The Prince's Trust. Sova is a charity working in the heart of communities in England and Wales, helping people steer clear of crime, stay out of trouble and build better lives. The Princes Trust has a mentoring scheme to help ex-offenders, start-up a new business. The mentoring interventions supported individuals in making the necessary changes to create a life free from criminality and enabled them to overcome personal barriers.

The evaluation of these mentoring interventions emphasised the key benefits that individuals developed, which included interpersonal skills and improved ability to identify their strengths, weaknesses, opportunities and threats. Individuals became more responsive in their thinking, creating solutions to problems and situations that led them away from a life of crime.

Additional research highlighted how businesses who engage in developing mentoring schemes, particularly within the company's growth period, are more likely to survive and succeed. I identified that a mentoring programme could help in the business development period as it is often a demanding time for all working there. My evaluations found mentoring relationships were mutually beneficial for the business and its employees.

I hope you will engage in the workbook's activities and use the text as a journey towards discovering how self-awareness and awareness of others coexist. Self-awareness plays a critical role in understanding ourselves and how we relate to others and the world at large. Being self-aware allows you to evaluate yourself in relation to your mentoring role.

Therefore, I encourage you to understand the importance of self-awareness in your position, whether work-based, freelance or volunteer. By exploring your current skills and learning how to use this workbook, you will find it will support you in your mentoring development.

This workbook serves the following purposes:
- It brings together thinking from a range of contexts where mentoring is used.
- It provides a theoretical framework to underpin mentoring development.
- It enables you to visualise distinctive and common ground between coaching and mentoring.

"Mentoring enables individuals to address fundamental challenges in adapting to business and interpersonal development." — Eileen Hutchinson

1-3 The overlap of coaching and mentoring

There is much debate about the differences between coaching and mentoring, explored more in my book "Understanding Coaching and Mentoring", (available via my websites or Amazon). Still, I found that some skills and concepts apply evenly to both, and the overview below lets you view these differences as two different activities, with the middle circle showing the overlaps. I hope you will value the uncomplicated visual impression and how it can aid you in your development.

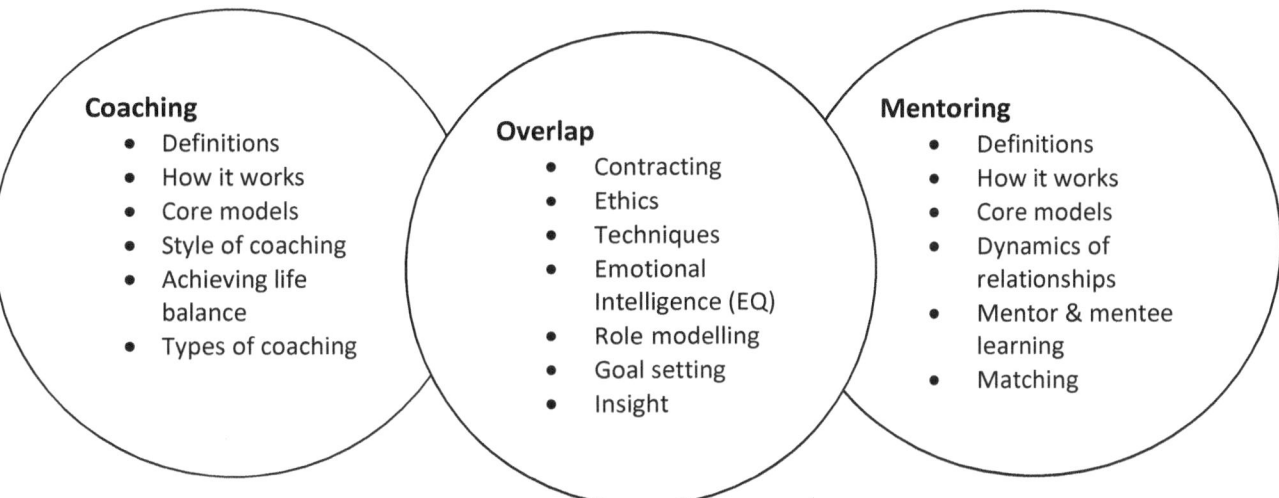

When I explored the differences between coaching and mentoring, it became apparent that some overlaps caused some confusion within the coaching and mentoring arena, which may impact the kind of training one should undertake to become an effective mentor or coach.

The visual aid presented is intended to encourage you to explore both practices' backgrounds, structures, and characteristics, including how the overlaps may influence your understanding of the nature of coaching and mentoring.

The middle circle identifies specific aspects of coaching and mentoring, including the need to discuss what is often referred to as the psychological contracting stage, which is done in the early stages of the coaching or mentoring relationship. The psychological stage is where each person agrees on their role, responsibilities, purpose, and sharing their expectations. This stage can never be overlooked as it is the foundation of the mentoring or coaching intervention, and when it is not discussed, the relationship can quickly break down.

I suggest you consider the questions posed in the middle circle before engaging in any form of mentoring and have your answers to these questions in place. By working through these exercises, you will develop a complete list of responses to clarify and understand the principal aspects of mentoring.

"Yesterday I was clever, so I wanted to change the world.
Today I am wise, so I am changing myself."
—*RUMI*

I would like to invite you to consider the following questions:
- Are you aware of the contracting elements of mentoring?
- Have you considered the ethics and competencies required?
- How is your EQ (emotional intelligence)?
- Who is your role model?
- How successful are you at goal setting?
- What insights have you developed so far in your life?

Please write-up your reflections here.

"Out beyond ideas of right and wrong, there is a field. I'll meet you there."
—*Rumi*

Task - Consider your current knowledge with relation to mentoring and make notes below to give you an understanding of what you know.

What is Mentoring?

How does it work?

What core models of mentoring are you aware of?

What are the benefits of mentoring?

Who would want to be mentored by you?

Would a mentor help you?

"A mentor is someone who sees more talent and ability within you, than you see in yourself, and helps bring it out of you." — Bob Proctor

1-4 The background to mentoring

The word 'mentor' comes from the Greek myth in which the legendary king Odysseus went off to fight in the Trojan Wars, entrusting his son's care to a friend called Mentor. The word means 'enduring' and is usually used to describe a sustained relationship between an experienced person and someone who is in the initial stages of their development. The word has become synonymous with the idea of a trusted adviser, a friend, teacher or wise person. The Oxford English Dictionary defines a mentor as an 'experienced and trusted adviser'.

The role of mentoring

Mentoring brings us all a new and dynamic way of relating and communicating to another person, i.e., the mentee. Many key characteristics add to the role of becoming a valuable mentor, including both the knowledge and experience of being supportive to others and a desire to share your experience to help others achieve in their life, career or business.

Of course, it goes without saying that a good mentor needs to have both high-quality listening, questioning and social skills, coupled with the ability to give confidence to their mentee, which is a crucial ingredient to be developed within the mentoring role. Another part of the mentor's role is to create an environment in which the mentee can feel both comfortable and safe, as this will encourage the mentee to focus on making their own decisions with an informed ability to take ownership of their life, career or business goals.

The role of mentoring is to provide support, encouragement and to offer help to the mentee so that they grow and develop as a person. Therefore, we can say that one of the roles of mentoring is to facilitate the mentee's interpersonal development so they can achieve their goals, dreams, and aims in life.

Developing the ability to offer an empathetic, calm supporting hand enables the process of learning to take place within the mentee's mind, and this shapes the way forward for the mentee to understand their strengths, weaknesses, abilities and potential. This is a crucial part of the mentoring relationship as it supports the mentee to move towards their desired goals. As a mentor, I suggest you consider using a gentle facilitation style of engaging and communicating with your mentee which will empower them to follow their aspirations and dreams and at the same time be able to offer guidance or counsel them as required.

Mentoring is a valuable personal development tool and is an appealing way of supporting yourself and supporting others to progress. It is important to remember that this is a partnership between two people, i.e., the mentor and the mentee, and is an equal, cooperative relationship based upon mutual trust and respect. As a mentor, you will be expected to guide and support the mentee to uncover the right pathway in life, and your role will be to expand the mentee's abilities, so they find their own solutions to the issues they are currently facing.

To become an effective mentor, you need to be on an equal footing with your mentee, i.e., having an equal relationship and avoiding any kind of power games, as any kind of games will be damaging to interactions and will leave all parties feeling negative about the relationship. Eric Berne's book "Games People Play" reviews the patterns of behaviour that reveal hidden feelings and emotions. For the purpose of developing the mentor/mentee relationship, you will need to expand your mentoring role around supporting the individual mentee rather than being task orientated.

"If I have seen further it is by standing on the shoulders of giants."
— *Isaac Newton*

As a mentor, you can expect to become a critical friend and a trusted guide who knows how to initiate and develop a framework around mutual respect. In many cases, the mentor brings a knowledge base and a lot of life experience, inspiring the mentee to progress in life.

The mentor brings many qualities to the relationship, including motivational and performance-related benefits. By this, I mean they can support the mentee with the ability to do things better, improve performance by refining behaviour and keeping the mentee on track by motivating them to stay focused and engaged in the mentoring relationship.

The mentor will need to challenge the mentee to consider taking actions, developing outcomes, and facing some of the obstacles they need to face for them to grow; this needs to be delivered in a non-judgmental way.

I invite you to review and consider a mentor's skills by studying the essential skills below. Make a note next to each of these skills as either having them or the need to develop:

- Equal relationship
- Supporting / Facilitating
- Individual support forms part of the working relationship
- Critical friend / Encourages development
- Trust (which is developed over time)
- Mutual respect
- Knowledge and experience
- Challenge / Problem solving
- Consistent
- Mutually agreed / Time, space and achievements.

Make a note of your key skills or the ones you need to develop.

"Everything should be made as simple as possible, but no simpler."
—*Albert Einstein*

1-5 The principal features of an effective mentor

An effective mentor's role and principal features are described as someone who is experienced within a particular field of work or sector and who takes a personal interest in offering support, encouragement, and guidance to individuals to gain insights into either personal or work-related issues. They hold regular meetings to maximise the success of the mentoring relationship, offering direction in interpersonal development.

Mentoring requires a fair use of emotional intelligence, which is often referred to as "EQ". You will need to understand and interpret the emotions or feelings of your mentee, both within the mentoring session and outside the sessions. It is essential for you to review how you see your "EQ" as your mentee may only share with you some aspects of their life and may not be able to open up to you with other factors or issues. So, as you can see, emotional intelligence plays a big part in developing a trusting relationship and supporting the mentee.

My top tips for developing mentoring relationships are:
1. Mentoring involves the development of a trusting confidential partnership that is founded on mutual respect.
2. Mentoring requires a commitment from both the mentor and mentee, without which nothing will be achieved.
3. The purpose of mentoring must be on an equal footing, with an agreement from both parties on the defined goals, agendas, outcomes and achievements.
4. Mentors will be seen as role models by their mentees; therefore, they need to provide good examples of behaviour, insights, understanding and, most importantly, to be just who they are, with no personas or masks.
5. Mentees need to show progress towards their achievements by taking ownership of the mentoring relationship, agendas, outcomes, and overall interpersonal development.
6. Mentors follow a heart-centred leadership model by providing value to their mentees which is done through integrity.

So, what is mentoring?

Having a mentor has been described as one of the most influential progressive relationships a person can experience. Yet you don't have to be an aspiring executive to benefit from mentoring. People from all walks of life can point out how a mentor has helped and supported them in either their career, life or business venture.

Mentoring plugs into a central theme that most other people share: the aspiration to pass on their learning to support other people to develop and fulfil their work-based or life skills. Developing a relationship with someone considerably more experienced does bring about incredible opportunities for growth and personal development.

A mentor is not there to tell a mentee what to do or how to behave, as this is down to the individual to decide what is right for them. However, they can discuss these issues, or if something is not working, then the mentoring relationship allows the mentee to contemplate these areas in a confidential environment, allowing them space and time to be open and honest with their mentor.

We all know that there are times when we all get stuck and feel emotional, and all you may need is someone to talk with, someone who has an open ear and an understanding of what you may be experiencing, and this is what mentoring offers.

As a mentor, I feel a wonderful sense of reward at seeing my mentees develop, and I'm always surprised by how they manage to take vast steps in changing their lives and social perspectives. I am aware that these life-changing occurrences may not have happened if individuals were not open to exploring their personal and working lives. As such, I feel mentoring offers a matrix of self-development opportunities and helps establish a range of interpersonal objectives and improves the mentee's performance in work and life.

I think it is the feeling of having someone behind you, their support, and the open, honest relationship (which may go on to become a friendship), which is quite a refreshing way to engage with your own development. You find yourself being open with each other, and the advice a mentee receives from the mentor can help the mentee make up their mind on what steps they want to take in life.

Mentees report how confident they have felt when making their own decisions and not second guess themselves anymore. Therefore, I have included some testimonials from people I have mentored. These are not included to promote myself as a mentor but to show you how powerful mentoring is. There is nothing better than hearing from the very people who have experienced effective mentoring.

David Edden - *"I recently completed business mentoring with Eileen and initially started the mentoring a bit apprehensively and didn't quite know what to expect, as I wasn't sure whether my business idea would be profitable and successful. After going through her mentoring programme and materials, not only did she hone and develop the different aspects of my business, but Eileen's encouragement, passion for business, knowledge and support was just what I needed to get going. The mentoring sessions were brilliant, and I have the tools to get going and get on my feet. I felt blessed and honoured to have met her and thank Eileen for her experience, enthusiasm, wisdom and encouragement".*

Heidi Setchtfield, PA Services - *"I had the pleasure of meeting Eileen recently on a Practical Skills for Business mentoring course. I went into the course not really knowing what to expect but passionate and confident about my business. Eileen's encouragement, knowledge and support was amazing, and I am so honoured to have had the pleasure of meeting her. I hope to work with her again in the future".*

Karen Jeffery Photographer - *"I started my journey with a passion but no idea and no confidence of how to take my business forward. I met Eileen on a business start-up mentoring course, where she took me under her wing and fuelled me with so much knowledge, confidence and woman power, she hasn't just changed my current and future career, she has put a strut in my step. Eileen isn't' just a mentor or coach, she is an amazing lady who mentors from her heart".* Thank you.

Dean Pierpont Business Growth Adviser: - *I was pleased to say that having Eileen as my mentor made the whole experience more enjoyable, Eileen was engaging, personable and very knowledgeable around the subject, if only all mentors and trainers could be like this then more people would undertake more personal and professional development.*

David Owen Business Owner - *Eileen is very passionate about achieving change through mentoring and coaching. She is able to determine the right balance between challenge and support and recognises the importance of humour in all aspects of her work. I can only recommend her very Highly!*

"You have to grow from the inside out."
— Swami Vivekanand

Task 1-1: Describe the role of an effective mentor - Considering your new mentoring role in supporting individuals, describe the essential parts of the work and the main activities.
Consider the definition of mentoring, the role of the mentor as distinct from other roles (e.g., trainer, coach, counsellor, therapist, supervisor, etc.), the focus of mentor in supporting individual development.

"Out beyond ideas of right and wrong, there is a field. I'll meet you there."
—*Rumi*

The principal features and benefits of mentoring

A mentor does not necessarily need to have been through the same experiences as the mentee; however, having a good understanding of the mentee's feelings is one of the most critical aspects of the mentoring relationship. Below I have outlined some of the principal features and benefits of mentoring, which you can consider when developing your mentoring practice.

As we now know, mentoring is the development of an equal relationship, particularly if you are a mentor in a senior position within the workplace. If this is the case, you may be seen as someone who is outwardly more experienced and knowledgeable, and this can, of course, put you on a pedestal as far as your mentee is concerned. Therefore, you need to ensure from the start that you have an equal relationship, as this is the only way that you can offer your mentee the opportunity to get the help, support and encouragement they need for them to gain the insights into who they are.

As a volunteer mentor, you have a lot to offer a mentee, and the different perspectives you have gained from your life experiences and situations may be of great benefit to the mentee. You may find yourself working with mentees from varied different backgrounds and, as the saying goes, "not one fit, fits all". With this in mind, all you need to do is be there for the mentee and keep an open mind and honest dialogue.

Working with The Prince's Trust as a volunteer business mentor enabled me to not only learn a great deal about my mentee's business goals, but I was able to research different areas of business development, enhancing my skill base too. As a mentor, you may find that you need to undertake research and acquire more knowledge to support your mentee, which is a good way for both of you to learn and grow together.

Working with Aspire (the international women's group) as a volunteer mentor, I found myself offering career development mentoring, which was a very different experience from offering business mentoring with The Prince's Trust. However, as I have experience working within a career guidance advisory role, I found myself falling into the mentoring role with ease. We explored many tools and techniques which enabled my mentee to move on in her career, and I have learned always to let my mentees set the agenda.

Confidence building

When we think of building someone's confidence, we are looking at the benefits of offering mentoring to someone lacking self-reliance or self-belief. Of course, this way of working will significantly impact anyone's life, let alone the mentee you will be supporting.

Confidence building helps facilitate the mentee's growth, and of course, a safe environment will be critical for the mentee to start taking risks and trying out new ways of thinking and behaving. Offering the mentee, the opportunity to understand themselves more and then by moving them towards the transition, i.e., the shift they want to bring about in their lives will enable the growth they are seeking to take place. Knowing and understanding that this process takes time is key to developing the mentee's confidence; therefore, patience is one interpersonal skill all mentors need.

As you begin building the mentee's confidence, you will see how they start to change the way they think about themselves and, once this process begins to take place, you will see their self-esteem becoming more in alignment with who they want to become. The acquirement of confidences always leads to the mentee becoming more motivated about the mentoring relationship, and it will enable them to bring about the changes they want to see in their personal and professional lives.

Stages towards mentoring success

In good mentoring relationships, the mentor supports the mentee to reflect on their own personal and professional knowledge, skills, and experiences. The mentor will share their own personal and professional experiences when it is appropriate. The psychology of learning informs us that there are four stages or steps to learning any subject, and here we look at the competence, or the "conscious competence" learning model, which relates to the psychological states involved in the process of progressing from incompetence to competence in a skill or behaviour.

The four stages suggest that individuals are initially unaware of how little they know or are unconscious of their incompetence. As they recognise their incompetence, they consciously acquire a skill and then intentionally use it. Eventually, the skill can be utilised without it being consciously thought through; the individual is said to have then acquired unconscious competence. The stages cover several elements, including helping someone "know what they don't know" or recognise a blind spot, which can be compared to some aspects of the Johari Window. However, Johari deals with self-awareness of blind spots, and the model below deals with the four stages of conscious learning.

The mentee's new self-awareness will happen at first on an unconscious level, and then you will find that it takes on its own momentum to becoming conscious. The conscious awareness will strengthen the mentee's self-belief and serve as a catalyst and an acknowledgement that they can make the changes they want in their lives. This will set the frame for developing the critical aspects of developing an effective mentoring relationship.

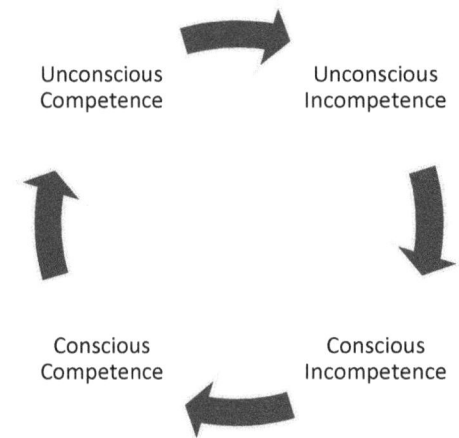

Shortcuts to mentoring mastery
- Keep motivated
- Manage chunks of work and learning
- Ensure a good emotional state is maintained
- Give knowledge time to become embedded in the learning process
- Teach the learning state and anchor the state in the mentoring sessions.

Stages towards success by being mentored are just like taking the steps above, and the process is what you can expect to happen within the mentoring journey. The four stages of learning provide a model for all learning and development. The model suggests that mentees are initially unaware of how little they know or unconscious of their incompetence. As they recognise their incompetence, they consciously acquire a skill and then deliberately use it. The mentee is said to acquire unconscious competence by working with their mentor. Eventually, the mentee will have moved through the process without it being a burden on them.

The principal features and two benefits of mentoring

Now let us consider the principal features and two benefits of mentoring. In order to help you understand and form your own opinions, please find below a few examples from my own experience and from people who have trained with me, and then move on to answering the questions set out in task exercise 1.2.

The features are described as:

- Helping the mentee develop interpersonal skills can assist in unblocking barriers or avoidance issues that an individual might be making by sabotaging their growth or success in either work or business.
- By providing a safe environment for the mentee to discuss interpersonal relationships, these issues can be overcome.
- Mentoring can help the growth of confidence on the mentee's part, resulting in more sustained changes than, say, increased confidence achieved through a short training course.
- Mentoring improves job performance through enhanced understanding and knowledge as it helps the mentee strengthen their communication skills and confidence to ask difficult questions.
- Mentoring improves self-awareness, job satisfaction and loyalty while supporting the development of new knowledge and skills.
- Mentoring improves acknowledgement for spotting and developing talent, which is a core fulfilment of human psychosocial needs.
- Mentoring progresses individual career development and opens new job opportunities within organisations.

Task 1-2: Describe how mentoring can benefit those being mentored in a range of situations - Outline the main benefits of the mentoring you are about to undertake by describing at least three situations where the mentoring will add value.

"There is no growth without guilt."
—*Bert Hellinger*

2-0 Barriers to effective mentoring and how to overcome them

Barriers to effective mentoring need to be overcome for the mentee to progress and achieve personal and professional goals. As we know, there is a range of factors that can be seen as a barrier and, as such, we need to be aware of what can go wrong and how we can make things work. The fear of being judged and the fear of failure can be two factors that get in the way of developing an effective mentoring relationship.

Mentoring is geared towards future paced action; mentors should support mentees to look to the future and recognise any possible obstacles, issues or risks that might prevent them from achieving their goals. To do this, mentees need to be able to express and explore potential problems before they happen. Some of the barriers may be emotional or cognitive, for example, low self-esteem or confidence to do the job. Neenan and Palmer (2001) refer to cognitive barriers as performance interfering thinking (PIT). We explore the psychology of mentoring on page 52.

One potential barrier can be a lack of time to devote to the mentoring activity, and this lack of time can come from either the mentor or mentee. For mentoring to be effective, it is vital that both parties can commit their time to get something out of the mentoring intervention. This barrier can be overcome by both parties agreeing at the start of the mentoring programme what the barriers are and how much time will be committed.

Another barrier could be the expectations of mentoring from the mentee's perspective, so this is where you need to be clear about your role as a mentor and where you may have limitations. If the mentee expects you to be the source of all knowledge and are the one person to sort out all their problems, you will find you have some issues to deal with, as no one person can fit this expectation.

Earlier I mentioned the importance of offering training to everyone on the mentoring programme. This allows individuals to understand what is expected of them, and it clears up any misconceptions around their roles and the mentoring intervention.

The IOEE Mentors code of conduct states that a mentor does not give advice but rather helps the mentee weigh up situations through reflection, questions, challenges, and feedback, allowing the mentee to come to a decision themselves. The mentor will conduct themselves with dignity and act in a way that respects diversity and promotes equal opportunities. Informing your mentee of the various codes of conduct should help them understand your role.

Understanding the capabilities, know-how, and techniques you need to be an effective mentor will provide a well-defined guide to the boundaries of a mentor's role. How you behave and show up as a mentor will also form the legal features and requirements of the role. Although it may feel uncomfortable, it is essential to discuss and agree on appropriate boundaries of how the mentoring relationship will function. If the boundaries are too loose, they are open to being misunderstood; on the other hand, when they are too inflexible, they may hamper the relationship.

Everybody, as we know, has different ideas about boundaries, from feeling comfortable with the physical environment, talking about personal matters, to the amount of time you need or want to spend with each other and the types of activities you will undertake. Therefore, it is essential to prepare to speak openly and honestly about both of your expectations, which, as you know, will vary in each mentoring relationship. Similarly, it is vital to ensure you are both on the same page about how you want to work together, so, as we can see boundaries need to be put in place, agreed on and form part of the contract.

Always bear in mind that mutual; trust and respect between you both are fundamental to the mentoring process and its function. In its code of ethics, the EMCC (the European Mentoring and Coaching Council) set out a statement for boundary management. This states that the coach/mentor will:

- At all-time operate within the limits of their own competency, recognise where that competence has the potential to be exceed and where necessary refer the client either to a more experience coach/mentor, or support the client in seeking the help of another professional such as a counsellor, psychotherapist, or business/financial advisor.

- Be aware of the potential for conflicts of interest of either a commercial or emotional nature to arise through the relationship and deal with them quickly and effectively to ensure there is not detriment to the client or sponsor.

Ensure you go through all aspects of your role and include this in the mentoring contract. As mentioned earlier, an outline of both roles will help overcome another potential barrier, where a mentee may demand too much of the mentor's time. If either party is unclear, it will act as a barrier. Therefore, defining roles before starting the programme and reviewing the relationship regularly will help overcome obstacles.

Having a sound plan in place with procedures that shape how you intend to progress, including resources required to support your mentoring arrangement and an approach that endorses what you are doing and why you are doing it, will add value.

Remember that managing the relationship does not mean that you must take charge; instead, it is more about being accountable and responsible for your role in the mentoring relationship. You both contribute to setting up the tone, meetings, and formal aspects of the mentoring plan.

Task 1-3: Identify potential barriers to effective mentoring - There are likely to be potential barriers which will affect the success of your mentoring. Outline two or more and explain why they are each a potential barrier.

Develop strategies to overcome barriers or obstacles
A mentor needs to identify with their mentee what the barriers or obstacles are, and this can only be done where there is trust within the relationship. Mentors need to encourage their mentees to think about potential resolutions to the barriers or obstacles they are facing. A mentor can do this by working with their mentee to develop an action plan or goal-focused strategy to overcome or reduce possible risks. Unlike PIT the mentor can help the mentee construct performance-enhancing thinking (PET) (Neenan and Palmer, 2001).

Rapport building plays an essential part in developing the relationship. It also helps the mentee overcome barriers and enables both of you to engage with each other fully. You will find this helps build the mentee's confidence, allowing them to respond to you openly. Building rapport gradually and patiently will help the mentee trust in you and your goodwill. Relationships develop easier by sharing values, ideas and includes how you both see the world.

You will know you have good rapport if:
- The mentee shows signs of positive body language.
- The discussions are energetic, lively, active and animated.
- The mentee is energised about what they have learned.
- The mentee is willing to explore with you concerns they consider to be uncomfortable.
- The mentee is empowered to take control of their development, life and career direction.

You both contribute to the mentoring contract by discussing:
- Confidentiality.
- What is important to you.
- When to phone, times to meet.
- The understanding of both roles.
- The time needed to invest in the programme.
- The responsibility for growing the relationship.
- Access to any documents used to record the sessions.
- The importance of feedback and that you are both open to giving and receiving feedback.

Remember, rapport building is about creating a safe place to discuss sensitive areas of the mentee's life; therefore, you should consider how you will build rapport throughout the mentoring journey, not just for the first few sessions. Creating a safe place is about ensuring you are both feeling comfortable with each other. You can do this by having a similar tone of voice, language, body movements and shared values or experiences. Building rapport is all about observing how the other person is responding to you. Using your insight and knowledge, you can look at how the mentee replies to your questions by noticing their body postures, i.e., are you both mirroring each other or cross-matching?

When you find yourself in the company of others, have a curious but subtle look at how people are acting and communicating with each together. Look for patterns of matching body language or other similarities between them. Other observations can be added to the list below, but the important thing is that you can see how this happens. You may want to use the following questions to guide you:

- Are their body postures similar?
- Do they mirror each other, or are they cross-matching?
- Look at their expressions; where do their eyes go when talking?
- Are their voices similar in tone and sound level?
- What does all this tell you?

How can you overcome barriers to the mentoring relationship?

In this task, as cited earlier, you need to consider how you will overcome any potential barriers and provide an explanation for each one. Considerations need to be given to the individual's needs, i.e., personality, any issues between those involved in the mentoring relationship. Learning and communication styles, educational background, and aspirations. Remember, it takes time and patience to help the mentee feel safe and confident to speak up, so you must persist with the relationship.

Another aspect is understanding the legal and ethical requirements relating to the role of a mentor, which may include equality and diversity, data protection, health, and safety. Therefore, you should refer to your mentoring organisation for specific guidance on the legislation relating to the mentoring activities. It is essential that you both have a complete awareness of what the role of a mentor/mentee really is.

EMCC (The European Mentoring and Coaching Council) state in their global code of ethics for Coaches, Mentors and Supervisions that the legal and statutory obligations and duties are:

3.11 Members are obliged to stay up to date and comply with - All relevant statutory requirements in the countries in which their professional work takes place. Safeguarding legislation when working with children or vulnerable adults. The relevant organisational policies and procedures of the work context.

3.12 Members will have the appropriate professional indemnity insurance to cover their coaching, mentoring and supervising work for the countries in which they operate and where such indemnity insurance is available.

Task 1-4: Explain how to overcome the potential barriers to effective mentoring - Provide an explanation of how to overcome each of the potential barriers to effective mentoring that you have identified.

"Giving up wanting to help or rescue people is essential if you sincerely respect them."
—Bert Hellinge

2-1 Defining the characteristics of effective mentoring

An effective mentor's characteristics and skills are vital to creating a good relationship, and of course, we need to display these characteristics for the mentee to engage in the process. When we think of a mentor's characteristics, we need to remember the difference between a skill that can be learned and the aspects of one's personality, one's character, which is pertaining to or indicating the qualities of a person.

Skills required by a mentor:
- Good communication and active listening - a mentor needs to question, explain, summarise, and give feedback.
- Self-awareness - knowing their strengths and weaknesses helps to improve the relationship with the mentee.
- Determining goals - a mentor needs to set and achieve their own goals to help the mentee do the same.
- Encouragement, support and trustworthiness - the mentor needs to cultivate a strong relationship with the mentee.
- Behavioural awareness – knowledge and understanding of another's behaviour.
- Business or professional know-how – insights into how things work around the office etc.
- Understanding and the ability to place issues in a broader context.
- Conceptual modelling – they have the curiosity and skills to ask questions to seek out and identify patterns in the topics they talk about with the mentee.
- Creating metaphors supports the mentee to understand better what is going on and how it needs to be changed.

Note, as a mentor; you will need to identify where you feel you have the skills and experience to support the mentee, as one of your many roles will be helping them develop their capabilities and interpersonal abilities. Depending on the challenges faced by the mentee, you may find that they need support in developing a range of social and business skills.

The characteristics to consider modelling are:
- The ability to build rapport with others.
- Understanding the importance of pacing and leading.
- Assisting with goal setting and celebrate achievements with the mentee.
- Demonstrating how to be a person of good moral with ethical principles.
- How to manage one's state, i.e., temperament, interaction, and responses to others.
- Have a keen interest in your learning - by developing and obtaining more knowledge to add to your own experience. You should also have a mentor or supervisor.
- Emotional Intelligence (EQ) – a mentor can see beyond the surface and quickly help the mentee do the same.

Encouraging an environment of trust within the relationship will help you and your mentee work through potential challenges. As we know, the mentor's goal is to build self-confidence and inspire the individual to become self-reliant. Accordingly, a good mentor Invests in their own self-awareness and development, supporting the mentee to look at gaps in their learning and experience; therefore, mentoring encourages individuals to be themselves and think proactively about their development and interpersonal ambitions.

"Your view of life all depends on the lens you are looking through."
—-*Eileen Hutchinson*

We need to include and review how empathy has become a crucial element of Emotional Intelligence. As a mentor, when you show empathy, you are making an effort to 'step into another person's shoes, i.e., your mentee. Becoming conscious of their feelings and thinking processes will help you see how their beliefs and values affect their view of life. Preparing yourself to see things from your mentee's perspective will develop the ability to become compassionate. I feel it is always better to talk with your mentee about their experiences than imagine how they might feel. This, I believe, will enable you to gather factual information rather than speculation.

Empathy is not about agreeing with your mentee; it means that you are willing to recognise and understand what they might be going through and see it from their perspective as mentioned above. Therefore, empathy supports you in understanding the needs of your mentee.

Appreciating that it takes time to become an effective mentor, it is essential to remember that displaying an understanding and compassionate attitude will help in developing the relationship. For me, it is about working from a place of deep understanding, I believe this is special as it creates greater empathy within the mentoring sessions. This approach offers a deeper level of mentoring, as it explores the emerging needs behind the mentee.

Compassion on its own doesn't make for being a good mentor, instead, it is one of several abilities a mentor needs to be effective in their role, particularly when developing the relationship, and you may find the following to be of benefit:
- clarity (offering clear communication and encouragement)
- capability (by sharing control of developing the relationship)
- compassion (where the mentee feels their mentor is "standing by them")
- consistency (the mentee knows what to expect from their mentor)

Task 2-1: List the key skills required to be an effective mentor - Consider the key skills you need to be effective in your role as a mentor. Present a minimum of two of these skills in a table which gives essential information about those skills.

"Once you get the lesson, whatever that may be, your life will improve."
—*Eileen Hutchinson*

2.2 Mentoring models

Every mentor or coach has their exclusive way of working, which offers value as they bring their unique style to the mentoring relationship. In essence, having a framework or model to work too will enhance the mentor and mentee's learning opportunities. Whatever model you use will need to be applied in the most discreet way to bring the best outcomes for the mentee. So, let's begin by reviewing some mentoring models, codes of ethics and additional resources. You may also want to undertake further research to understand each model thoroughly.

The European and Mentoring Coaching Council (EMCC) inform us that *"Our aim is to define, create and promote best practice for all in mentoring and coaching. For professionals in the field, we provide a reference point for key elements like standards and ethics and a continuous conversation about how to keep improving them".* (https://www.emccuk.org),

The Coaching and Mentoring Network expresses through their website the need to connect you with providers of personal, professional and organisational development services, as well as free information and resources about coaching and mentoring. They say: *"Our community is drawn from a wide range of backgrounds, and all are committed to professionalism and respect for the diversity and equality of good practice that exists within the dynamic field of mentoring and coaching".* (http://new.coachingnetwork.org.uk)

Mentoring, as we see, can stretch employees supporting them to perform even better through exposure to high performing colleagues or external mentors. Therefore, a mentor must have knowledge and experience in working with different mentoring tools, techniques, and models, which assist the mentoring relationship in having a clear sense of direction. The effective mentor must demonstrate considerable flexibility in responding to individuals' learning styles, so the matching process requires careful consideration.

A structured approach is one of the main factors in the success of mentoring schemes (Arnot & Sparrow, 20024). The conversation may focus on the person's learning. Still, it will be most effective when it also involves an awareness of their learning strategies, blocks to learning, feelings about their learning styles and an understanding of how mentoring models can support the mentoring process.

Once an appropriate mentor has been chosen and there is an agreement in place with the mentee, you can start to look at how the mentoring practice and models will work. Therefore, it is essential to understand, and be aware, that the mentee may not necessarily know what goals they are aiming for or indeed where to start, and this is where a mentoring model can help.

Influential mentors almost always follow a pattern or model of discussion by starting or re-establishing the relationship with an informal check-in before probing the mentee about what they would like to discuss. They never jump in with information before going through the stages of getting the facts as the mentee sees them. An effective mentor will understand the benefits of working through a mentoring model with their mentee.

The role is to structure the mentoring conversation by moving the other person through the stages of a mentoring model, tool, or technique. The structure of any model ensures reflection on the activity at the outset, moving on to planning and future actions being taken.

"The delicate balance of mentoring someone is not creating them in your own image but giving them the opportunity to create themselves." — **Steven Spielberg**

Before you decide on the mentoring model you are going to use it is useful to remember that there are three basic types of communication: words, tone of voice and body language. What percentage of these three types do you believe the average person uses? Note these down below and the answer can be found on page 30.

- Words %
- Tone of voice %
- Body language%
- Total

One of the coaching models, which is now also being used within the mentoring field, is the GROW model, established in the 1980s by the late Sir John Whitmore and partners. The Grow model will help the mentee discover their own solutions around what they want or need to do.

GROW stands for:
- **G**oals, which must be SMART.
- **R**eality of the situation.
- **O**ptions/Obstacles.
- **W**ill to act on a way forward.

Over the years this model has been modified and reshaped, 'growing' in its own development.

The GROW model raises an individual's awareness and understanding of:
- Their own aspirations.
- Their current situation and beliefs.
- The possibilities and resources open to them.
- The actions they want to take to achieve their personal and professional goals.

Setting goals that are inspiring, challenging, specific, measurable, and achievable, in a realistic time frame enables the GROW model to successfully promote confidence and self-motivation, leading to increased productivity and personal satisfaction. The Will element of the fourth stage in the model is the barometer of success. It relates to decisions, desire, and intention. Model adapted by Eileen Hutchinson

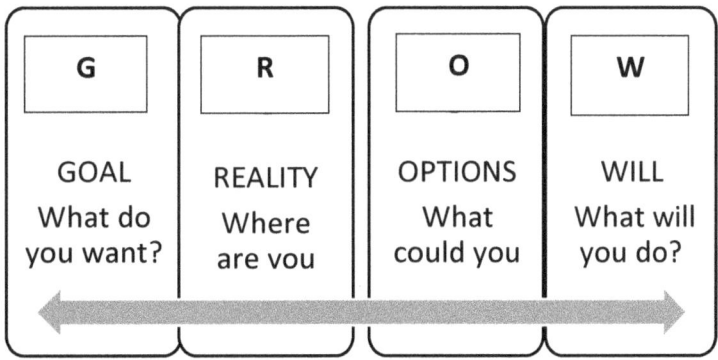

"If you always do what you've always done, you will always get what you've always got."
—*Author unknow*

CLEAR model of mentoring

The CLEAR model was formulated in the early 1980s by Professor of Leadership Peter Hawkins of Bath Consultancy Group. Although the CLEAR model preceded the popular GROW model developed during the 1990s, it is still considered a functional alternative for managers and coaches. CLEAR operates under the idea that to achieve maximum workplace performance, it is no longer enough to be just a manager – directing and orchestrating actions – you must often intervene in staff processes and act as a catalyst, or a guide, to their development. The model places a strong emphasis on the need for coaching and mentoring in today's fast and competitive business environment to promote employee growth. Model adapted by Eileen Hutchinson

The CLEAR model acronym stands for:

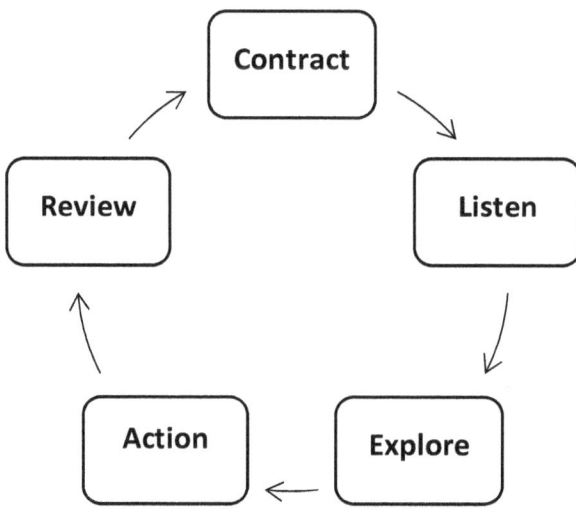

The CEDAR feedback model

The CEDAR feedback model is a five-stage feedback process that is heavily influenced by coaching. The model provides space for the recipient to speak and includes a stage for follow up. The stages are Context, Examples, Diagnosis, Actions and Review.

- Clarify – Clarify the context of the situation and behaviours.
- Explain - Explain the situation and give examples of performance and observed behaviours.
- Discuss - the situation to understand the difference between expected and observed behaviours.
- Action – Take action by agreeing on plans for improvement with timelines.
- Review – Review the progress made and amend plans if necessary.

These models are based on the core principle that the ownership of results is with the mentee. Therefore, the models or processes act as a framework to support a positive and productive conversation between mentor and mentee. The mentee is given the opportunity to build self-confidence from deciding what they need to do, as mentioned above, rather than being told what to do.

"It is generally accepted that words account for 7%, Tone of voice about 38%, and Body Language for about 55% of communication."

Using a mentoring model such as the GROW, CLEAR or CEDAR, will support the mentee with the setting of goals. Using the SMART model below alongside the models' goal aspect will ensure you are both working toward an achievable outcome, the SMART outcome.

The acronym of SMART stands for:
- **Specific** – what does the mentee want to achieve?
- **Measurable** – so that progress can be reviewed and tracked.
- **Achievable** – not impossible, it needs to be a target, i.e., something to aim for, which is not out of reach.
- **Relevant** – the mentee needs to understand how it will help.
- **Time-bound** – there needs to be a time frame for it to be achieved.

Specific
- Clear communication to those contributing to the achievement of the goal, so misunderstandings are minimised.
- Visibly written, leaving little room for doubt or uncertainty.
- Typically stating an outcome and not merely an activity.

Measurable
- Monitor progress and make changes if necessary.
- Wherever possible calculated risks, which are discussed and worthwhile.
- Ability to look at other resources to help review the actions taken.

Achievable
- Challenging and interesting - exciting wherever possible.
- Consistent with available resources, i.e., budgets and people's skills.
- Serve as a motivational and a developmental tool for the mentee.

Relevant
- Have a real desire to offer support to the mentee.
- Be within the mentor's specialist area, which is relevant to the mentee.
- Developmental goals, to allow the mentee to move towards them.

Time-bound
- Indicate target dates (start and end), milestones, timescales or deadlines.
- Where a specific timescale is not applicable, a statement such as at all times, in accordance with laid down procedures, should be used.

The SMART is an acronym for the 5 elements of specific, measurable, achievable, relevant and time-bound goals. Smart goals are well-defined and focused, and a goal without a measurable outcome is like a sports competition without a scoreboard or scorekeeper.

Working with your mentees on their goals is such an essential part of the mentoring relationship. I would like you to consider any examples of developing SMART goals you may have in your mentoring toolkit and use them within your mentoring role.

What are your SMART goals for becoming a mentor? Are they:
- Increase professional knowledge and training?
- Improve low-functioning work processes or relationships?
- Have new experiences?
- Attain a leadership role?

The INSIGHT cycle of coaching and mentoring

The INSIGHT cycle of coaching and mentoring was redeveloped and redesigned since co-authoring Understanding Coaching and Mentoring. I based the INSIGHT process on my extensive experience of mentoring, coaching, teaching and research. You will find this book is theoretical, and it is a good reference book for anyone undertaking a higher-level study programme in coaching or mentoring, particularly at Levels 5 or 7 or in Management or Executive Mentoring.

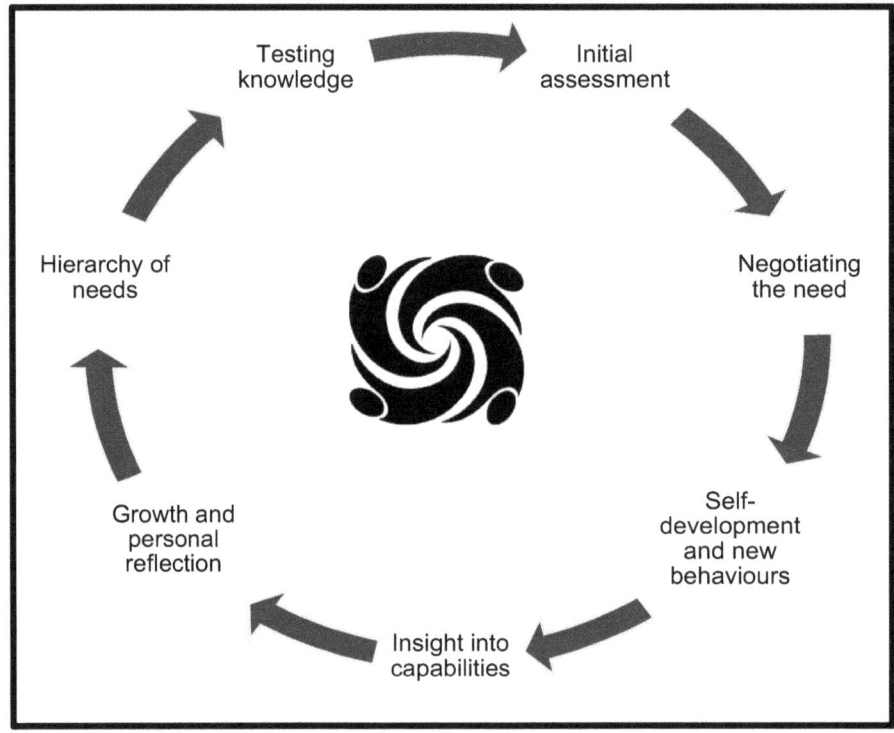

The INSIGHT cycle of mentoring gives a framework for mentoring meetings and will help the mentee plan a way forward. The themes shown allow you to identify several vital interventions that need to be well-thought-out when working with mentees.

The benefits of using this model are two-fold: it enables you to move towards being a first-class mentor while supporting you to demonstrate the strength of character, transparency and ability to develop meaningful relationships based on sincere and honest dialogue. This model will equip you to challenge perceptions, attitudes and behaviours in a safe and secure environment. Coaching and mentoring demand a multifaceted skill set, and hands-on experience is essential.

Looking at and contemplating how I worked as a mentor enabled me to create a model that directly reflected how I engaged with individuals and how the sessions worked. The cycle and the acronym INSIGHT represent what actually happens in a coaching or mentoring process, and the model is an excellent way to start working with individuals.

The benefits of using the model when you start your mentoring practice will give you a frame to deliver an entire cycle of mentoring.

> *"Mentoring is a brain to pick, an ear to listen, and a push in the right direction."*
> *— John Crosby*

How to use the INSIGHT coaching and mentoring cycle

I - Initial assessment
The initial assessment will give you the opportunity to build rapport with the coachee/mentee whilst eliciting the core requirements for the coaching/mentoring intervention.

N - Negotiating the coaching/mentoring plan
Negotiating the coaching plan is a key component of the INSIGHT cycle, covering environment, ethical practice, preparation, time commitment and paperwork.

S - Self-development and new behaviours
The self-development plan or CPD (continuous personal development) will enable the coachee/mentee to identify areas for development, it will afford the coach/mentor the opportunity to suggest and discuss new behaviour techniques or new learning with the purpose of bringing about personal change.

I - Insight into own capabilities
Once the coachee/mentee engages in the first part of the INSIGHT cycle they will identify and discover insights into their own capabilities, including reviewing both their strengths and weaknesses, allowing for a deeper understanding of their personal beliefs, values and goals.

G – Growth and personal reflection
The growth and personal reflection period will give the coachee/mentee the time to reflect on the interventions provided with the view to monitor, review and evaluate what has worked well and what may need to be modified.

H – Hierarchy of needs
This element of the cycle will give both parties insight into the motivation and achievements to date, ensuring the basic needs of the coaching/mentoring intervention have been completed before moving on to discussing more complex needs.

T – Testing new skills and knowledge
The testing stage will give the coachee/mentee time to test their new skills and knowledge (within their work and lives), while gaining a deeper appreciation for their personal and professional achievements.

The essence of good mentoring, using this model, is that the development process is two-way and depends on the two parties having absolute trust in each other. Here are some tips and insightful questions that you could ask the person you are coaching in each stage.

My model is referenced in two academic texts "The Little Book of Coaching Models" by Professor Bob Bates and "The Little Big Book of Management Theories" by Bob Bates and James McGrath. How to use it – Reference "The Little Big Book of Management Theories" published by PERSONS (my model is on page 86 model 36). "The INSIGHT model is relatively straightforward and the process of talking an inward-looking perspective and reflection is a good way of thinking about the model.

"Pacing a key skill to master when mentoring."
—Eileen Hutchinson

The constituents of the model can be summarised as:

Initial assessment: This will give the mentee the opportunity to elicit the core requirements for the mentoring intervention.

Negotiating the coaching plan: This should cover important aspects of 'what?' 'when?' 'where?' 'how?' the intervention process will operate.

Self-development plan: This will enable the person being mentored to identify areas for personal or professional development and enable the mentee to discuss appropriate mentoring approaches that will support their development.

Insight into own capabilities: This will encourage the individual to review their strengths and weaknesses.

Growth and personal reflection: This is an opportunity for both the person being mentored and the mentor to reflect on the interventions so far and evaluate what's worked well and what needs to be modified.

Hierarchy of needs: This will give both the person being mentored and the mentor insight into whether the needs of both parties are being met.

Testing new skills and knowledge: This will give the individuals the opportunity to test new skills and knowledge and make assessments about what else needs doing.

- Determine what the individual wants by asking: "What specifically do you want to achieve by working with me? What counts as success to you? What style of mentoring do you respond to best?
- Clarify how, when and where mentoring will operate by asking the individual: "Where do you feel most comfortable learning? How do you see the client-mentor relationship developing?
- Identify what areas for development are available by asking them: "What are your current strengths and weaknesses? What are the opportunities and threats facing you?
- Gain a deeper understanding into the individual's beliefs, values and goals by asking: "What do you believe that you will do differently as a result of the mentoring? How will you know when you have achieved this step?
- Confirm that the individual is on the right course by asking: "What are you doing to make the changes happen? What are the effects that the changes have had?
- Establish that their needs are being met by asking: "What effects have the changes had? What do you think will change next?"
- Establish that their needs are being met by asking: "How comfortable do you feel with what's happening to you? How would you assess your motivation, and do you want to carry on?
- Confirm that the individual has achieved their desired outcome by asking: "What are the main things you have learned from the mentoring? How do you intend applying the learning?

Questions to ask yourself:
Am I asking insightful questions?
Am I getting honest answers to these questions?

How to use it – Reference, "The Little Big Book of Management Theories", written by James McGrath and Bob Bates, published by PERSONS (my model is on page 86 Theory 36). Use this when you want to have a framework for supporting people to move forward.

Eileen Hutchinson and Richard Hale claim that the benefits of using the INSIGHT Coaching/Mentoring cycle will support the coach/mentor to achieve the strength of character and transparency to develop an influential relationship with the person they are coaching based on sincere and honest dialogue. The authors go on to say, that using this model will enable a coach/mentor to challenge perception attitudes and behaviours in a relatively safe and secure manner.

I am delighted my model is referenced in both of these books as, when I was writing the INSIGHTS book with Dr Richard Hale, I wanted to express how my work has enabled people to make major breakthroughs in their lives, careers and businesses. I wanted to help people understand how coaching/mentoring can enable individuals to get real results, and I feel this is what my model achieves. The creation of the model came about by my commitment to how I work with individuals and how passionate I am about encouraging people to grow through personal development.

In my latest book Effective Coaching, I have included a template for using the INSIGHT Cycle, as both mentoring and coaching are structured and focused processes. The template builds on the ideas by Professor Bob Bates, and it gives you a more insightful way of working with mentees or coachees. I felt it essential to explain the stages of the INSIGHT Cycle and how it can help you as a mentor or coach.

The cycle is a question-driven activity, providing you with a way to develop meaningful conversations that supports you and the individual to engage in the mentoring/coaching plan fully and is designed to help you deliver a complete mentoring or coaching programme.

The Stages.
Each stage of the cycle begins with a conversation about how that particular phase will work and in what way it will support you both to engage in the session. The testing stage will give the individual time to experiment with new skills and knowledge while gaining a deeper appreciation for their personal and professional achievements.

The Questions.
Each question covers the enquiry you might consider using with your mentee. The examples support you in looking at and focusing on the outcomes of the sessions. The testing questions: *"What are the main things you learned from the sessions? How do you intend to apply the learning? How will you measure the effectiveness of this,"* Giving the individual the opportunity to reflect, review and realise the impact and outcomes of their actions.

The Developments.
Each stage asks you to explore how the process is working, in what way you are both thinking about the sessions, how the individual is becoming self-aware, the impact of the tools and techniques and the importance of the mentoring relationship. The development testing stage will allow the individual to complete the programme or initiate additional sessions with a new plan. *"This is where the coachee can start to put in place a reflective way of thinking and discuss what has worked well for them or what they need to add or change; they could decide on a new approach or new goal or goals." Pg 62 Effective Coaching Eileen Hutchinson.*

The 5 E's cycle

I then moved on to developing my next model "The 5E's model", shown on page 35 This was created from reflecting on the INSIGHTS model and after working with a large number of mentees and coachees. The model will help you to set a frame for any kind of interpersonal intervention.

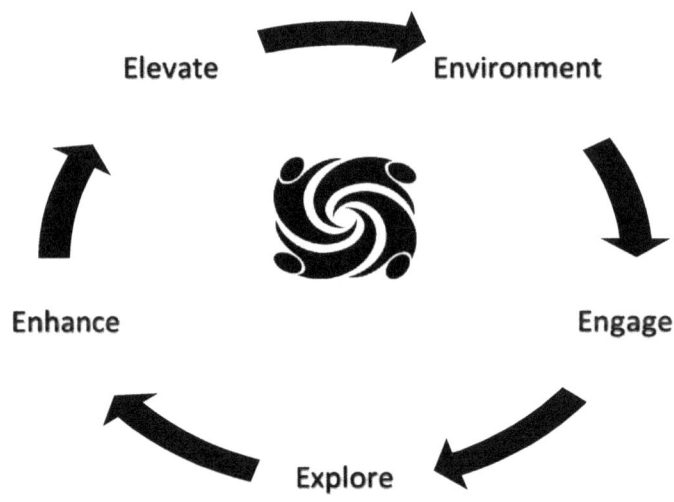

The 5 E's learning model can be used when working within the field of leadership, coaching and mentoring. The model is recognised to support and enable individuals to engage in personal development and become more effective. The 5 E's methodology is referenced by other professionals, universities, government bodies and educational institutions within the UK as publicised by the Peer-to-Peer training. The model allows you to learn and test many additional techniques and tools, helping you to create insight, awareness and to define goals.

The 5 E's model supports you to plan and elevate you towards a higher level of self-actualisation. The model will enhance your learning and help you create new ways of looking at barriers and developing solutions to your issues or problems. Individuals undertaking this programme find the 5 E's to be a powerful enabling tool, yielding accelerated results. I will publish a book on this model later in my career, but for now, let's look at how the model's process can support the mentee in engaging in the mentoring relationship.

The steps below show how important it is to create a safe space for the mentee to feel secure, enabling you to examine situations from a new and different perspective.

- Step 1 to Step 2 enables the mentee to engage in the mentoring sessions, and you will find they begin to try out new ideas during this stage.
- Step 3 supports the mentee in opening up to exploring their inner world, and they will start to learn how to respond to situations authentically.
- Step 4 takes the mentee on a journey towards state management and interpersonal improvement.
- Step 5 is where the mentee gains control of how they learn, communicate and engage with the world around them. This empowers the mentee to let go of old habits and create new ways of achieving their outcomes.

The 5 E's cycle further explored

Mentoring is a fantastic way to stimulate ideas and solve problems or issues by gaining a deeper perspective of interpersonal development. It can assist in achieving goals and objectives by looking at pressing and long-term aims, including those that stretch individuals. Using the 5E's model, you can offer the mentee the opportunity to deal with the broader background of their personal life, business or career. The outline below shows how each stage supports the mentoring intervention.

- **Step 1 Environment** – Self Awareness is the first step toward making changes that benefit you. This step is about the individual's self-awareness. By being self-aware, we can review how we behave and interact with others, which puts the mentee in a better position to evaluate and adapt their interpersonal development where necessary. Therefore, it is essential to create a safe space allowing the mentee the freedom to examine situations from a new and different perspective, which can only be achieved by them feeling safe and secure.

- **Step 2 Engage** – Self-development is the second step in shifting from reactiveness to responsiveness that can move you out of early attachment patterns to a more secure style if required. This is where the mentee moves on to feeling comfortable in engaging, learning and testing new techniques, tools, and models. This step supports you both in creating insight and awareness of how to define goals. Once the mentee starts to know and understand their personality and early attachment patterns, they gain the core requirement of progressing from self-awareness to self-development. *You can read more on attachment patterns and styles in my book Understanding Life Coaching.*

- **Step 3 Explore** – Awareness of potential is the third step in recognising you have the capability to develop into something in the future: This step supports the mentee with exploring how to be authentic by connecting with their inner-self. Exploring how certain questions, situations and people make them feel will help the mentee gain the tools to influence and modify their behaviour—allowing them to develop their potential and giving responses that are representative of their needs.

- **Step 4 Enhance** – Relationship management is the fourth step towards understanding your emotional state and the emotional state of others. This step accelerates interpersonal development by encouraging the mentee to challenge and increase their awareness of others. Once the mentee develops an open and curious mindset, they can utilise the tools and techniques learned. This step supports the mentee in building successful relationships within both their business and social activities.

- **Step 5 Elevate** – Emotional maturity is the fifth step in helping us cope with life by being resourceful and creating the conditions for success. This step builds on the previous four stages and will help the mentee move on to removing self-limiting beliefs and sweep away old patterns of behaviour, advancing to a higher level of self-actualisation, which is described as becoming "fully human."

"My mentor said, 'Let's go do it,' not 'You go do it.' How powerful when someone says, Let's do it together."— Jim Rohn

2-3 Mentoring compared to other developmental styles

We know that the essential components for mentoring relationships and programmes are understanding shared common interest and the clarity around expected roles, responsibilities, behaviours, and results. One of the difficulties with instigating mentoring programmes, particularly for worldwide groups, is working within different cultures. Individuals have different perceptions of what is involved, and this will need to be monitored. We have looked at various models of mentoring, and I would now like to include the basic styles of helping, which are:

Directive – This involves coaching but in a direct rather than passive sense, i.e., if your mentee says they are going to put their hand in the fire, what do you think? Here you would be directive – a directive approach involves a transfer of wisdom, where the mentor provides coaching advice or direction, probably based on their experience and expertise; this is a widely recognised and traditional approach.

Nurturing – This is about providing thoughtful, kind support and additional emotional care. So, you can expect to find yourself nurturing a person within the mentoring role by focussing on their personal development, guiding them towards taking the proper steps or actions and allowing them to make their own mistakes.

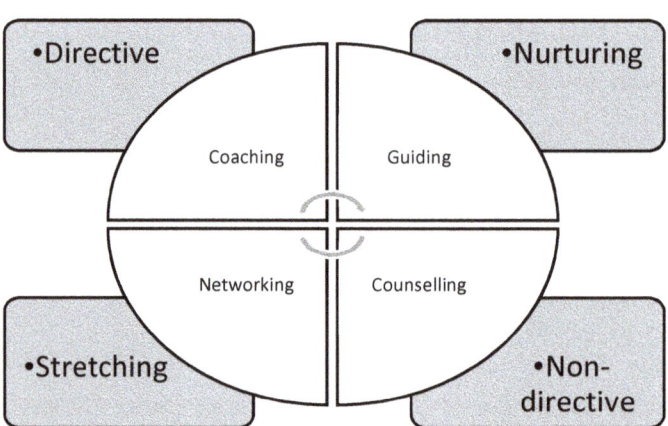

Stretching – This move towards providing opportunities for the mentee by encouraging them to network or networking on their behalf to open up opportunities.

Non-directive mentoring is when the mentee takes key accountability for developing the relationship, covering content, scheduling, direction and plan. In a directive relationship, the mentor directs the mentee towards explicit goals and gives solid advice and recommendations. In contrast, in a non-directive relationship, the mentor encourages the mentee to come to their own conclusion.

Counselling – This seeks to explore the underlying dynamics of individuals and their relationships. Counsellors and coaches both ask questions, but counsellors tend not to address tasks and performance issues. The model above highlights how mentoring compares to other developmental models and shows the vast skills needed to become an effective mentor.

The link below will take you to an interesting article on – emerging dilemmas and challenges for mentors and mentees in the new context for training in-service teaching, for the learning and skills sector, article by Sue Cullimore and Jonathan Simmons, the University of the West of England, Bristol. http://www.leeds.ac.uk/educol/documents/

2-4 Understand how to use different questioning and listening techniques

The mentor should have reasonable knowledge and experience of using a variety of questioning techniques. These include using open and closed questions and using the four W's – why, what, when and who.

Open questions will allow the mentee to fully relate to their thoughts, ambitions, feelings and develop a deeper understanding of their current situation and how best to progress. The mentor needs to use a range of questions and listening techniques to facilitate this process.

Closed questions would be used to ascertain the more challenging facts from the mentee (such a name, past job roles, ambitions, etc.), which will form the bedrock for outlining plans and moving forward, along with all the soft facts ascertained by the open questions.

Other questions to consider using are:
- Curious questioning.
- Funnel questioning.
- Clarifying questions.
- Probing, but not intrusive, questions.

Listening skills are also vital in developing effective communication – if you cannot listen fully, communication will be easily misunderstood. As we know, communication is a two-way process, and effective mentors understand how to listen correctly, how to pay attention to what is being said by both verbal and nonverbal communication.

I suggest you listen with curiosity to help you build a picture of the mentee's world, its information and its substance, and the mentee's experience of living in their world. Listen to how they define themselves and how they see their own potential, growth, and any obstacles they are currently facing. This will involve listening to and interpreting what your mentees are saying and noticing what is not being said. Therefore, it is essential to recognise both verbal and nonverbal messages when you communicate with your mentee.

Listening is an active process involving:
- Ears – for verbal communications.
- Eyes – for nonverbal communications.
- Body – for physically showing that you are listening.

Always practise active listening when you are mentoring. At a face-to-face mentoring session, sit square to and directly opposite your mentee. Turning at an angle from them will lessen your involvement. Adopt an open posture with your arms relaxed and your palms upwards. Lean slightly forwards to show that you are very interested in them and what they are saying. The mentee must see that you are comfortable and in control of the situation for them to feel secure.

Acknowledge your mentee and confirm that you are listening by using encouraging noises such as "I see", "Mmm", "Yes", and "Aha". These allow the mentee to continue talking with the understanding that you are listening to them. During face-to-face sessions, use these noises in conjunction with nonverbal signals, such as nodding the head and looking expectant.

Well-timed pauses give time for explanation, evaluation and development of thought. Be sensitive to facial expressions, which will help you understand the difference between a pregnant pause or an embarrassed silence.

Pauses on the telephone need to be continuously monitored so that your mentee does not feel that they must ask if you are still listening. Using active listening techniques will encourage your mentee to confide in you, allowing you to develop the relationship further than they ever thought possible.

Active listening techniques are essential to understand and master, especially if you want to become an effective mentor. I would like you to explore some of the methods on the next page and make notes alongside each one to further your understanding. When we encouragingly listen to others, we show interest and keep the other person talking. For you to do this, you don't agree or disagree with what is being said; you use neutral words and vary your tone of voice to match or encourage the mentee to talk freely, i.e. "Can you go on?", "I see", "Good point", etc.

Active listening creates a frame for you and the mentee to go a little deeper into the mentor/mentee relationship. Active listening means you learn to pay attention to your mentee by being fully present with them. It offers the mentee the opportunity not only to be listened to but also to be heard. Jenny Rogers book Coaching Practice refers to the Coaches Training Institute framework on Listening, which I feel is also related to mentoring. In this framework they state that there are 3 levels of listening:

Level 1- You are thinking of yourself, not the client, perhaps rehearsing what to say next.
Level 2- You are intently listening to the conversation and will hear what is not being said.
Level 3- Also described as 'radio-field listening.' You are operating at level 2, but also of the emotion, and risk what might be possible to take into the conversation. You feel connected to the client and can trust your intuition.

Clarifying is used to help you understand what the mentee has said – it enables you to gain information to help open new interpretations, and you need to ask questions here to get the mentee to clarify what has been said, i.e. "Can you clarify this?", "Do you mean?" "Is this still the main issue?".

Restating is done to show you are listening and understanding the facts of what is being said. It is used to check out meaning and interpretations by repeating ideas and points, i.e. "So, you would like your line manager to listen more", "So, what you mean is".

Reflecting is used to show you understand the mentee's feelings. It is done to encourage the mentee to reflect on his or her emotions, i.e. "You felt that this undermined your position", "You felt you didn't get a fair interview", etc.

Summarising is used to review the position that the mentee finds him or herself in. It pulls together significant points and prepares the ground for further discussions. It helps to restate ideas and feelings, i.e. "These seem to be the main points so far", "So this is the way you reacted to the situation".

Validating is used to acknowledge and confirm the other person's worthiness by recognising the value of their issues and feelings. It affirms what has been positive in their endeavours and actions, i.e. "It was good of you to think of your Mum at such a time", "I think you have done very well to stick with that training course."

You may be interested to read a blog on my website "The Promise That Changes Everything by Nancy Kline. I found this book to offer a fresh, new perspective on how to create a thinking environment. www.eileenhutchinson.com

"If you cannot see where you are going, ask someone who has been there before."
— J Loren Norris

2.5 Principal features of giving feedback and developing trust

Once we have learned how to listen and ask good questions, we will need to provide feedback to our mentee on what we have heard and observed; this should be done in an open, non-judgmental manner. Giving and receiving feedback is critical for someone to progress in their personal or professional development or make behavioural changes, which is a delicate and sensitive practice. You must approach this task with a complete understanding of the person's feelings as this will prevent the mentee from becoming defensive.

The feedback sandwich is most often used for both mentoring and coaching; the frame is to open with a) Compliment, b) Look at what needs to be addressed, changed, or further insights into behavioural areas, c) end with a positive.
- First positive point.
- Something to improve.
- Second positive point.

Mentoring responsibilities can be a little nerve-wracking at first, mainly because this kind of commitment is new to you. You suddenly find that not only are you responsible for your development, but you now have some responsibility for the support and development of your mentee. Having this broader remit and dealing with it effectively will always boil down to building a positive relationship with your mentee. As you know, the best way of building effective relationships with others is to open up and maintain effective communication lines.

The art of feedback is the ability to communicate and effectively receive information so that the mentee can achieve the dual purpose of feedback, which is motivation and development. Feedback is a process that helps your mentee to reflect and focus on what they are achieving, why they need to achieve it and how they are going about achieving it. Feedback may be well-defined as information about past behaviour and actions delivered in the present, influencing future behaviour and actions. The word feedback can have negative connotations for some people. Just think how you would feel if someone says, "Do you mind if I give you some feedback?" You are probably waiting to hear the list of things you are doing wrong or waiting to defend yourself against the other person's incorrect perceptions.

As a mentor, you must ensure that feedback is not perceived negatively and as a disapproving exercise. If feedback is concerned with others' behaviour and actions, it is also concerned with the behaviour and actions of yourself. The tone and atmosphere you create in giving feedback will often determine how effective and positive it will be. Feedback will need to be balanced and constructive if it is to address the aims of being motivational and developmental.

Feedback Matrix

The feedback review model is a simple 2×2 matrix mapping feedback activity. Positive feedback should be celebrated if expected or unexpected. Even if the feedback is negative, using this kind of matrix will enable you to look at the mentee's understanding, knowledge, emotional IQ, state management, and fears.

Expected	Unexpected
Positive	Negative

Developing trust

Developing trust in the mentoring relationship is such an essential feature as it will create the core conditions for trust to emerge. You need to consider how you will create an environment in which the mentee can feel safe. We know it takes time to develop and build trust in any relationship, and therefore it should be no different in the mentoring relationship.

Trust develops because of the mentor's skills and actions, so the mentor needs to be reliable, patient, encouraging and responsive. The mentor should also give honest feedback and use listening and questioning techniques to gain the mentee's trust.

Key principles in developing and building trust:
a. Ensure you take the time to know and understand your mentee. Make time to talk about their life outside of the business. Try to know what they think and why. Value their perspective even if it is different from yours.
b. Do what you say you're going to do. Decide on what they and you aim to achieve throughout the mentoring sessions. Be consistent and always do what you say you are going to do.
c. Communicate openly and honestly. Discuss concerns as soon as they occur, ask for and give feedback.
d. Maintain your competence. Frequently evaluate your professional and personal development by continuously training, mentoring or supervision, update your (CPD).
e. Demonstrate compassion but don't be frightened to challenge. An open, honest relationship means you can challenge positively, which will support your mentee to explore a broader perspective.

Relationships need to be built before any effective mentoring can take place. An environment of trust and mutuality must be established. It is essential for the mentor and mentee to become acquainted with each other (Kutilek & Earnest, 2001; Mincemoyer & Thomson, 1998).

1. Begin each relationship with a getting-to-know-you-session.
2. The mentor should greet the mentee warmly and help the mentee identify their professional needs and goals.
3. The mentor should learn about the mentee's educational background and experience and share information about their background and experience.
4. The mentor can then continue to build upon the mentee's strengths, needs, and goals throughout the mentoring period.

Integrity is an essential aspect of a mentor role, as individuals who do what they say they are going to do encourage trust. Mentors mostly demonstrate their integrity by the way they uphold confidentially. So do individuals who speak honestly about their thoughts, feelings, and life experiences and whose actions mirror their principles. All these elements are vital to building trust within the mentoring relationship.

Consider the following points when answering the questions on trust- role modelling, creating a relationship based on mutual respect, demonstrating own experience or credentials, setting expectations and empowering others, setting boundaries within the relationship, sources of support and referral, the importance of confidentiality and situations when information may need to be shared.

"Making someone else feel special is a gift to share."
— Eileen Hutchinson

3-0 How to organise mentoring activities

When it comes to organising mentoring activities, one needs to consider how to plan for practical sessions. The first point of call is to ensure that you have set aside enough time to carry out the session. The importance of limiting interruptions during the session will depend on the meeting place. It is essential to give your full attention to the mentee throughout the time you spend together. This will contribute to creating an environment where trust will start to develop.

The other considerations are how to review the intervention, and this is where mentoring records need to be incorporated into the planning process. Maintaining mentoring records is vitally important as it allows for objectives and goals to be recorded, which can help the mentee focus on what is needed from them. Keeping mentoring records is also an excellent way to track a mentee's progress as they become motivated to achieve more.

The question is asking you to explain how to plan for mentoring sessions. Describe methods that would be used, including questionnaires or forms, to assess the needs of individuals being mentored and any agreements required between the mentor and the individual (mentee). Also, consider where and when mentoring takes place so that mentoring is appropriate to the individual and their situation.

You may wish to look at the 5E's model to understand how the right environment creates a safe space giving individuals the freedom to be themselves. This generates a psychological acceptance of the current situation they find themselves in, opens up new ways for the mentee to express themselves, and examines concerns from a new and different perspective. Once this state is achieved, you can progress with your mentee towards how they want to work and explore the mentoring contract and future goals.

Points to consider when planning for mentoring sessions. Assessing needs and use of questionnaires Or forms, identifying gaps in skills, attitudes, or behaviours, planning for mentoring discussions and mentoring agreements. The following is an example of a checklist covering points you might find useful to discuss at your first meeting.

The list is taken from the NWDA Solutions for Business mentoring:
- What do we expect to learn from each other?
- When will we check the relationship is working for us?
- How will we end our relationship if it isn't working?
- What are our goals and what is the order of priority?
- How will we measure progress?
- Do we both agree the openness and trust are essential?
- Will we both give honest and timely feedback?
- What is the ideal schedule for our contact and meetings?
- How will we meet?
- How long shall we meet for?
- Will either of us take notes?
- What can we record?
- What will we agree about boundaries and confidentiality?
- To what extend is each of us prepared to share our network of contacts?
- What is the agenda for our next meeting?

"Life, the greatest teacher we have."
—*Eileen Hutchinson*

Mentoring is about having a logical way forward or - put it another way - a clear sense of direction as mentioned earlier. As a mentor, you need to help the mentee establish clear goals or several small goals. If we only think about goals, they are only "thoughts", so you need to help the mentee take action to achieve their aims.

Some questions to consider are:

- What do you want to accomplish?
- What do you want to be different in your personal or professional life?
- How long do you have, what is your timeline?
- What skills would you like to develop?
- What has stopped you in the past
- If you could change one thing, what would it be?

It may take time before the mentee is ready and clear about what they want to achieve. The mentor's part in the relationship is to support the mentee to develop goals, and patience will be needed. Using the SMART goal planning tool can help you as it is a very useful tool, and it gives the mentee Specific, Measurable, Achievable, Realistic and Time-bound objectives to work on.

Remember, the mentoring relationship is an energetic and recurring activity. The relationship is constantly evolving, moving towards a successful or a series of successful outcomes; therefore, the relationship takes time to build. Understanding the various stages of the relationship's development supports the mentee to achieve their goals and, as such, balances and supports the mentoring process to bring about the essential ingredients for positive mentoring intervention.

When you find yourself in the mentoring role, you need to be sensitive towards your mentee. Mentoring is a delicate process, not a reactive relationship, so emotional intelligence plays a huge part. Awareness of the mentee's hopes, dreams, and desires is essential. Being aware of the barriers they face and have faced is ultimately the best way to help the mentee overcome obstacles and setbacks. Therefore, their individual goals need to be discussed, reviewed, and amended throughout the relationship.

I describe the relationship as *"a more experienced colleague shares their knowledge to support the development of an inexperienced team member of staff, to support the departmental performance."*
However, a mentoring relationship is more informal and long-term and unlikely to involve any performance monitoring. There is no accountability on the mentor regarding whether the mentoring sessions have achieved measurable goals or targets.

According to Mumford, mentoring is *"a protected relationship, in which experimentation, exchange and learning can occur and skills, knowledge and insight can be developed."* (Mumford (1993). All staff undertake mentoring training to ensure we equip them with key mentoring skills to impact on the business's ongoing development and success. We have found a mentoring culture is essential for developing responsive thinking, creativity and links into the team and departmental performance.

"One of the greatest values of mentors is the ability to see ahead what others cannot see and to help them navigate a course to their destination."
— John C. Maxwell

3-1 Mentoring records

The purpose of record keeping is to improve the goals between sessions and enable you and the mentee to look at how you undertook planning, evaluation, progress and any amendments that needed to be made. Records provide the mentee with some notes for review and support them to move towards their goals and be able to review their sessions. This gives the mentee a record that shows clarity of understanding, a description of what was agreed, and how other actions have helped the mentee progress.

Mentoring records need to comply with the Data Protection Act and the new GDPR Act, as well as the code of practice for mentoring, which states that "Mentoring is a confidential activity". You should have, or you will need to set up, a policy covering what is expected of both parties and a duty of care towards the mentee, which is to be followed by the mentor. The mentor's overall responsibility is to act in such a way as to support the developmental needs of the mentee.

You will use different kinds of records to support the mentee throughout the mentoring process. By developing a system that enables you to maintain appropriate records, you will benefit from the mentoring programme reviews. Still, the overall benefit is for you both to review the mentoring relationship. This is an essential aspect of the mentoring intervention as the records document the journey of the association between you and your mentee. They also outline the progress made towards the mentee's achievements or serve as a way for the mentee to review the initial steps towards their goals.

If you run a mentoring programme on behalf of a third party, both the mentor and mentee must respect the third parties and staff involvement. For the sessions to be successful, the mentee will always have access to any notes taken about them, as this gives the relationship the equal footing needed for the intervention's success. The records need to show enough support has been provided to the mentee, highlighting how the mentee has taken ownership of the mentoring activity, including goals, progress, and actions. You need to ensure the records are maintained and completed correctly.

You will need to explain what records are required when mentoring an individual,
the importance of record keeping and what should be included, i.e.

- Data protection,
- Confidentiality,
- Assessment,
- Using a mentoring diary to consider progress of individual and own performance as a mentor.
- Example records can be provided to illustrate your descriptions.
- Describe how to keep records of individual mentoring sessions.

The use of preparation forms will allow you both to review and document important aspects of the mentoring programme. The following is an outline from the prep forms I use with mentees, and it is a great way to introduce reflective learning as a practice.

1. What have I achieved since our last session?
2. What didn't I get done but intended to?
3. The most beneficial aspect of our last session and how have I applied it?
4. The challenges and problems I'm facing now?
5. I want to use the mentor during the next session to?

3-2 Practical application of developing mentoring skills

Having looked at the skills to use in mentoring sessions, you are now faced with the task of undertaking mentoring for the practical elements of achieving the qualification outlined below.

Undertake at least three hours of mentoring:
- You must provide evidence that an individual has been correctly and appropriately mentored for at least three hours over more than one mentoring session.
- This will typically be in the form of a diary or log.
- Particular reference should be made in the diary to the following:
- You should use appropriate and correct questioning and listening techniques to support the mentoring role. You should give examples of this within your records of mentoring activity or reflections. Alternatively, your tutor may cover the assessment of these in your supervised mentoring session.

Points to consider;

You should give appropriate and correct feedback to a mentee to support their development. You should provide examples of this within your records of mentoring activity or reflections. Alternatively, your tutor may cover the assessment of these in your supervised mentoring session.

You should identify and use correctly and appropriately two or more behaviours designed to develop trust in the mentoring relationship. You should give examples of this within your records of mentoring activity or reflections. Alternatively, your tutor may cover the assessment of these in your supervised mentoring session.

You should accurately maintain and submit as part of your diary complete and appropriate records of your mentoring activity including goals, progress and actions.

You should complete detailed and appropriate reviews of your mentoring performance after each mentoring session. You should provide evidence of at least a one-hour mentoring supervision meeting with your tutor.

You should identify two or more areas for future improvements in mentoring skills based on your own mentoring performance reviews and your mentoring supervision meeting.

Good mentors are characterised by their ability to provide the right kind of help when it is needed. They also view the mentoring relationship as one where they can learn too. I have provided a checklist below for you to consider the kind of help or support your mentees may need. Review the list and if helpful create your own list.

Mentees will find a mentor of most significant help if they:
- Need to understand things that aren't easily explained in a book or manual.
- Are willing to be stretched and challenged, as well as supported in achieving personal goals.
- See the value of tapping into someone else's broader/more significant experience.
- Are prepared to work with the mentor to develop mutual new learning.
- Want to develop a whole range of additional learning resources for themselves through more effective learning.
- Have long-term goals which will require them to grow in many ways, some of which may not be immediately clear.

3-3 The matching process

Matching mentors with mentees are one of the most critical and core activities for implementing and managing mentoring programmes. Without a good matching process, the mentoring relationship could prove pointless. For the programme to be successful, you will need a framework around which the mentoring interventions will work.

Mentors are matched with mentees based on reasons such as how the mentor's experience reflects the mentee's desired achievements, which can be gained through further development and greater capability. The mentor is usually more senior than the mentee and can champion or advocate for the mentee within the organisation, or it could be a volunteer mentoring role, one where the mentor has an interest and relevant experience to support the mentee.

Some groups take a freewheeling style and let mentor/mentee relationships develop without much thought on how the matching process will be managed. They only offer the mentor/mentee support as a token hoping the relationship will grow. Other groups will take a proactive approach, using clear objectives and principles to match the mentor with the mentee. The assessment process around the pairing is included within the programme. This is usually achieved by employing a mentoring specialist or training an employee or employees to undertake the task.

There are several factors you need to think about when matching mentors and mentees within a mentoring scheme. Matching can become tricky at times, particularly when participants in the programme do not clearly understand how mentoring should work. The matching process must fit in with the vision, values, and overall objectives of the group. If individuals want to choose their own mentee to mentor, you will be offering the freewheeling approach, which may cause you more pain in the long run; therefore, planning the matching criteria with care is a must.

Here are five tips to get your mentoring programme off to a great start:
1. **Identify the objectives for the mentoring intervention** - There are various reasons you are involved in the mentoring programme. The purposes might be for career or leadership development.
2. **Identify the specific reasons you are offering a mentoring service.** For example, if the aim is to provide career development to employees, you want to make sure you match mentees with mentors at their next logical career level.
3. **The application process** - Consider how you will go about getting the mentee's needs and the mentor's expertise matched at the right level.
4. **The matching process** - Consider how you are going to match mentors with mentees. For example, a mentee could pick their own mentor or be assigned a mentor from the programme administrator.
5. **After matching, ensure the mentorship will be successful** - There needs to be a way of guaranteeing the mentor and mentee receive all the help and resources they need. Provide enough training to both parties, so each knows their role in the relationship.

According to Johnson (2002), The mentor and mentee pairing is one of the most critical steps in any mentoring relationship. It needs to be managed appropriately. The pairing of the mentor and mentee is not to be taken lightly. Researchers typically define the pathway by which a mentor-mentee pair develops as either (1) informal mentorship or (2) formal mentorship.

"Small achievable goals can bring incredible results."
― *Eileen Hutchinson*

3-4 The role of supervision in mentoring

Mentoring is all about supporting others, and therefore we need to be sure we are working in an ethical way and supervision, as part of any mentoring programme, is essential.

Participating in supervision is a way for companies to safeguard their investment and maximise the ROI of mentoring in their business. By engaging in supervision, organisations are much more likely to establish and maintain mentoring practices, offering them a long-term solution. Organisations that create transparent processes for their mentoring supervision programmes will have a much better understanding of the impact of getting it right.

Mentoring supervision connects the gaps and joins the dots between theory and practice. A mentor can use their supervision sessions to focus on actual issues that occur in the mentoring relationship, which will support personal development. The mentoring method is growing, so it is vitally essential for mentors to continue their professional development after gaining any qualification.

Why do you need a supervisor - First and foremost, a supervisor can help the mentor to develop expertise in professional areas. Having the opportunity to reflect on your work and talk through tricky issues and what has worked well allows you to explore different approaches to help your mentee's development. A supervisor can help the mentor become more explicit in how their own perceptions influence situations and whether they approach the issues that work best for their mentee, ensuring professional mentoring standards are followed. Supervision plays a vital role in helping people to explore how they operate as mentors.

Many professional bodies such as APECS, the ICF, The Association for Coaching, the EMCC, CIPD and ILM are now encouraging and advocating supervision. A supervisor should sit outside the mentoring programme or the business; an independent supervisor with the experience of offering supervision is ideal for providing supervision for mentors.

The supervision process will give you time and space to reflect on your practice, and you will have a chance to gain objectivity and put some kind of perspective on your work. Supervision also provides you with the ability to reflect on the processes and outcomes achieved and experiment with new ways of creating shifts for your mentee. There are different ways to engage in supervision, and here we look at the most popular ones.

One-to-one supervision - Personal one-to-one supervision allows you to explore your practice as a professional regularly, either face to face or by video conferencing. In essence, the supervision process's purpose is to offer a safe space and the opportunity for individuals to engage in thoughtful reflection, raise concerns, explore problems, uncover new ways of handling situations, and reflect on responses. A central feature of supervision lies in its potential to exercise and review best practice.

Group supervision - During group supervision, you can expect to work with several practitioners from various professional backgrounds, including the corporate, public and mental health sectors. Group supervision will offer you the opportunity to gain support in the form of ideas, information and suggestions from other professionals, as well as emotional support and appropriate reassurance.

The importance of receiving regular supervision can also be seen as part of your CPD (continuing professional development). Increasingly, HR departments and buyers of the helping performance and training professions request that their external coaches, mentors, NLP practitioners, and trainers be in regular supervision. This gives the company the chance to maximise its ROI (return on any investment).

Group supervision, like one-to-one supervision, will enhance your ability to review and evaluate the mentoring progress by giving you the space to reflect on your mentoring practice and look at your individual qualities.

As a mentoring supervisor, I have outlined my supervision programme below

Supervision, as part of the Continuing Professional Development (CPD) of any mentor, is essential. But for internal mentors trained within an organisational context, it is of paramount importance. Regardless of whether the organisation has one internal mentor or a sizeable internal function, supervision will be critical to the future success of mentoring inside the organisation.

Investing in supervision is a way for organisations to protect their investment and maximise the ROI of mentoring in their organisation. By understanding both mentoring and supervision outcomes, organisations are much more likely to establish and sustain mentoring practices in the long term. Organisations that establish clear measures for their mentoring supervision programmes will better understand the commercial impact of getting it right and the damage that can be done if they get it wrong.

Mentoring supervision bridges the gap between theory and practice.

A mentor can use their supervision sessions to be mentored on real and specific issues to further their personal development. Additionally, suppose a mentor reaches an impasse with their mentee. In that case, they can refer to their supervisor to learn new tools and techniques or refresh existing skills and practise them in a safe environment.

A supervisor can help the mentor become more explicit on how their perceptions influence how they approach a situation and whether that approach is beneficial for themselves, their mentees, the organisations they work for, and whether it adheres to professional mentoring standards. Here, the supervisor acts as an independent third party to help the mentor maintain balance and objectivity, even in difficult situations. Supervision plays a vital role in assisting people in exploring how they operate as mentors. Supervision sessions give the mentor the chance to vent their frustrations and to talk about problems.

The practice of mentoring is evolving all the time, so it is crucially essential for mentors to continue their professional development post qualification. Reports show that many mentors participate in private research, networking and attending conferences but far fewer benefit from short courses, formal training and further education. In terms of personal development, there is much more emphasis on theory than on practical application. As a supervisor, I work to the standards of ILM and the EMCC Supervision Competency Framework. EMCC supports the use of competence frameworks as part of a broader approach to the training, development and assessment of coaches, mentors and supervisors. https://www.emccglobal.org/quality/supervision/

Mentoring supervision is a place for you to reflect on your work and continue with your professional development. Supervision is a collaborative learning practice which will continually support you to build your mentoring capacity". Please visit my website for more information on supervision. Finally, an external supervisor provides the opportunity to work towards a standard by measuring and assessing the mentoring service against the organisation's objectives, offering a form of quality assurance.

"We make a living by what we get, we make a life by what we give."
—*Winston Churchill*

3-5 Ending the mentoring relationship

The mentoring journey takes you and your mentees on a deep dive into their lives and their aspirations. You learn about each other, and the stories of your mentee's life play out like a movie or a book full of different chapters, different experiences and people. Like any good story, it will start with a beginning, including a middle and have a natural ending. The whole process of the relationship links into narrative mentoring, and by this, I mean most people tell their life stories through their own lens and how they see their own life, and they may use metaphors to tell the stories that have shaped their lives.

In my mentoring and leadership training, I introduce the topic of metaphors as they are used in our daily conversations. Metaphors are the words or phrases that individuals relate to when they want to describe an object or action to which there is no literal relation. I recall one of the times when I used a metaphor with a mentee. I used the metaphor because the mentee was not taking responsibility or completing the tasks they had agreed to, which would eventually move them forward in their life. We had been working on these tasks for a long time. It was when everything else seemed to be failing, and I seemed to be running out of ways to continually motivate my mentee that we had the most significant and most insightful breakthrough.

My metaphor at the time was, *"You can take a horse to water, but you cannot make it drink."* I was a little concerned that I might have overstepped the mark here, as I was not sure how it would land, but it made all the difference to the mentee. The next session amazed me as my mentee had made many changes and achieved many of the goals that she had been procrastinating about; she told me that when I had said the metaphor, it was like a light switch had gone on in her mind. So, metaphors can be helpful, but you must use them carefully.

Since that session, I know that metaphors in mentoring can be used as keys to understand the stories being told to you by your mentee. You can use metaphors to get a deeper understanding of your mentee's life or give them the insight they seek, as I did above. You may find the words or metaphors used in the mentoring sessions occasionally include what the mentee wants to tell you but somehow struggles to find the words. Therefore, by using metaphors, you can open up their communication skills and enable them to say what they actually mean. The more you listen to the narrative of the mentee's life, the further you can use the tools of metaphors to gain clarity and develop clear outcomes.

When you 'spot' a metaphor used by your mentee, you can help them by paying attention, exploring the meaning behind the metaphor and understanding its importance? A compelling method of questioning has been developed by psychologist David Grove called 'Clean Language'. Clean language means your language is 'clean' because you say nothing to taint the mentee's perception. You merely direct their attention towards the metaphor and the shapes and symbols that evolve from it. If this is a new area of self-development, I suggest you read metaphors in mind, which will give you a deeper understanding of the process.

Penny Tompkins and James Lawley took David Grove's process and developed it into a coaching model and other therapeutic uses. They call it "Symbolic Modelling". It is a modelling process because, through specific questions, you are attempting to 'replicate' the mentee's experience in your mind. I work with clean language in my mentoring and training sessions, but before you set out to use this process, may I suggest you engage with a mentor or coach experienced in the procedure or undertake training.

When you start the mentoring intervention, you need to have an end in sight; this is why the mentoring contract should contain clear notes on what has or has not been achieved. Good notes give you a record of what has been accomplished, reframed and appraised at the end of each session.

It covers what was set out initially and whether the expectations were realistic and will show you how you both explored other options and made appropriate changes. The end of the mentoring process will be a time to review the experience and hopefully celebrate success.

Therefore, discussing and planning for how you will end the relationship is essential. When we start talking about the end of a mentoring relationship, we can design and agree on the timescale. Consequently, when it comes to the end of the scheduled programme, you can discuss the ending and clarify if there are any outstanding goals or if you need to change the timeline.

As you move towards the ending of each mentoring relationship, you are all given a chance to get together to understand what the mentoring scheme has accomplished. All stakeholders will have a different mentoring programme experience, and each area will have outcomes that cross over each other. However, you will all gain from reflecting on the original objectives and reminding yourselves of the benefits to the mentee.

Where the mentoring scheme has proper launches, with a clear start and end date, closure can be accomplished appropriately. Good mentoring schemes adhere to and follow specific ways of closing down, and here I have included a few ideas for you to consider.
- Keep the mentee informed that the end date is in sight. It is always good to have a timeframe to support the mentee, so 4 to 6 sessions ahead of time is a good benchmark to consider.
- Give the mentee the proper mentoring materials to review, i.e., the records you have contributed to throughout the sessions.
- Consider and explore the possibilities of continuing the mentoring relationship with your mentee. You may find that they would like to engage with a different mentor and, if so, you can then close your mentoring part of the scheme with them and pass them on to the coordinator. Whatever the outcome, for you, the relationship with them will come to a successful end.
- Remember to celebrate the relationship and what you have both achieved.
- If appropriate, ascertain whether the mentee would like to consider becoming a mentor themselves. If so, pass them or their details on to the coordinator or scheme manager so they can move forward in the mentoring role.

Closing the session
When you have both agreed on the session's final date, you might want to consider having the session in a different place. The last session with your mentee may be filled with mixed emotions on both parts, so remember to ask how they feel and be honest with yourself; again, you can run through this area with your mentor.

Use the session as an opportunity to recap and remind yourselves of the goals set at the beginning. You might want to explore any other support your mentee might need and discuss whether you will stay in touch. One of the main things I've learnt from being a mentor is setting clear boundaries to ensure that everybody's expectations are managed. I think that's important from the beginning and helps you approach the ending so you're both on the same page.

When I work with groups or organisations to develop and implement their mentoring programmes, I include a training package for the mentors, mentees, and mentoring managers. This enables everyone involved to have a clear overview of the mentoring scheme and will contain the benefits of mentoring, what the mentor/mentee wants to achieve and what they are looking for in the mentor/mentee relationship. It also gives a framework for understanding expectations and if support is needed outside of the relationship.

4-0 The psychology of mentoring

Mentors come from varied backgrounds and have different life experiences. Although we do not need a degree in psychology to become a mentor, we need to understand the psychological principles on which the practice is based. Without this understanding or training in mentoring, you may risk not achieving the intended outcomes from delivering mentoring sessions.

Throughout the workbook, I have focused on the development of practical skills to become an effective mentor. At this point in your mentoring journey, it is essential to discuss the psychology of mentoring, as without this understanding (mentors may) fail to achieve the intended results.

The psychology of mentoring means your mentee feels safe, involved, and able to perform to their potential. It also means they feel comfortable enough to raise any interpersonal concerns they may have with you. Mentoring is not merely a complementary practice; it is a process that is fully integrated throughout the learning journey. On a psychological level, it effectively meets the mentees personal, social (wellbeing) and learning needs.

The psychology of mentoring doesn't need to be a daunting topic, nor do you need to remember word for word how it works or what to say when becoming a mentor. It is, however, good to understand how the process works from a mentee's perspective, which I have tried to incorporate throughout the workbook.

As you work with your mentee, you will help them identify their hidden skills and latent talents; this means the mentoring process becomes productive in developing the mentoring relationship. Positive psychology works best when your mentee feels involved and is broadening their knowledge and skillset. This only happens when you are focusing on their needs or the problems they are facing. Remember moving your mentee towards a positive mindset needs to be done with patience and skill.

Mentorship is an opportunity for you to help change a mentees outlook on life, i.e., from what is not working to what is working in their life or career. Change is not something that everybody adjusts to, particularly in the early stages of the mentoring relationship so again patience is required.

A good book to read is "The Psychology of Coaching, Mentoring and Learning" it provides a thorough understanding of the rationale, theory and practice of coaching and mentoring from a psychological perspective. Ho Law, Sara Ireland and Zulfi Hussain unify the psychology underpinning this diverse and expanding field, then demonstrate how both individuals and organisations can easily apply the principles and techniques of coaching and mentoring. A wide range of tools and exercises are provided to implement the techniques described.

There have been vast amounts of research into "resistance to change" and "change management". According to the SGCP survey, the most common approaches are cognitive and behavioural, with over 60% majority (Palmer & Whybrow., 2004). While NLP has gained popularity in life coaching, it is the least used technique among professional psychologists.

I would like to give some background information on a valuable tool linking to the psychology of mentoring, CBT (cognitive behavioural therapy), developed by Aaron Temkin Beck, a psychiatrist working in the United States in the 1960s and 1970s. The research he undertook was based on the link between emotion, cognition, and behavioural intervention. His observations discussed how individuals preoccupied with their emotional thoughts tend to talk to themselves (the so-called internal dialogue); at this stage, CBT was shaped.

CBT belongs to the facilitative mentoring style in that mentors do not provide mentees with immediate solutions to their problems. It is also congruent with the psychology of learning approaches advocated in this workbook. In this context, mentoring is regarded as a collaborative process. Mentors help build a platform to guide and support the mentee to discover their inner strengths and plan a way forward.

CBT aims to support you in dealing with overwhelming problems in a more positive way by breaking them down into smaller parts. Therefore, CBT is based on the concept that our thoughts, feelings, physical sensations, and actions are interconnected, and that negative thoughts and feelings can trap us in a vicious cycle. In my mentoring sessions, I use CBT to show mentees how to change these negative patterns to improve the way they feel by focusing on current problems rather than focusing on issues from the past as we look for practical ways to enhance the mentee's state of mind daily.

I studied NLP many years ago and incorporate the skills and processes within my mentoring sessions. I support my mentees with tools that support and enhance how they engage and communicate with themselves and others. NLP helps us to manage ourselves in a more congruent manner leading us to live an authentic and enriching life. NLP is the practice of understanding how people organise their thinking, feelings, language, and behaviour to produce their results.

NLP provides people with a methodology to model the performances they want to achieve. NLP is also used for personal development and for success in business. A key element of NLP is in how we form our unique internal mental maps of the world as a product of the way we filter and perceive information absorbed through our five senses from the world around us. The theoretical underpinning of NLP is covered in my workbook "Understanding NLP Coaching"; however, it is good to note that NLP can be a helpful tool to use within the mentoring role too.

Action learning advocates an optimistic mentoring style based on people coming together as peers in a 'learning set' and supporting each other in tackling work-based problems using a question-based approach. On occasion, peers may be able to provide specific technical advice about solving problems or developing particular skills; however, the power of the peer mentoring approach is more in line with the idea of asking insightful and thought-provoking questions of each other.

Mentoring, as we see, can change people's lives, and I know of many mentors who have faced difficulties or obstacles and now use these experiences when appropriate to share with their mentees, but one needs to know when to share and when to hold back. It is essential that you continue developing your skills, which can be achieved by either engaging in training, supervision or being mentored yourself.

On page 54 you will see a case study example of my work with Hertfordshire University where I developed an effective Peer to Peer mentoring programme for the mental health sector, this programme involved using all of the aforementioned tools and techniques and they were introduced in a delicate manner over a period of sixteen weeks.

I hope this brief overview gives you an understanding of how positive psychology can provide a foundation to improve the quality of your mentoring practice. As a mentor, you will go on a personal journey, and I encourage you to engage in interpersonal development and that you have the appetite for learning more about the psychology of mentoring, CBT, NLP and Action learning sets.

"People grow well when they learn to love and appreciate who they are."
—Eileen Hutchinson

4-1 Case studies and templates

When writing the INSIGHTS book on coaching and mentoring, I included some case studies, and I would like to reference one of these in this part of the wordbook. The case study below is an example of how mentoring/coaching can enable people to make empowering changes in their lives and links back to the psychology of mentoring.

Case example - The Mental Health Sector; Peer coaching and mentoring - I was asked by the University of Hertfordshire to research peer mentoring and how it may help people within the mental health sector. From my research findings, I developed and pioneered a highly effective peer-to-peer coaching and mentoring programme delivered to Mind Network, Guideposts Trust, Viewpoint, and Dens in Hertfordshire. This programme is now run nationally by Mind.

The course was written and delivered by me and accredited by ILM (The Institute of Leadership and Management). Students opted for either the endorsed or development award in mentoring, which depended on their educational level. Subjects included: Goal setting, Motivation; Managing the relationship, and well-formed outcomes.

The training was delivered to a mixture of staff, volunteers and clients. Upon completing the training, the clients progressed to becoming volunteer mentors. This progression plan helped individuals move on to the next step in making a considerable change in how they perceived themselves. In Hertfordshire, we now have a pool of mentors who mentor others to make positive changes in their lives and overcome some of their mental health issues. Supervision formed part of the initiative, and the training outcomes have changed people's lives. It was a very personal experience, and people who suffered from low self-esteem gained new insights into their emotional and behavioural problems and made incredible progress.

Testimonial – Manager, Guideposts Watford, Hertfordshire, UK. *"The Mentoring and coaching came at just the right time for our organisation – the courses have helped staff, volunteers and clients to support each other at a more constructive level than previously and have helped some individuals' confidence enormously. I particularly think that the goal setting and some of the techniques, such as looking at the different areas of your own life, fit into our holistic approach."* The overall message we can take from this case study is the importance of individuals coming to the mentoring sessions with a sense of openness.

My research has informed me that individuals drive effective learning, and when individuals have an element of control over their learning experience, the outcome becomes more effective. The methodology I worked with was process-driven; I mean, individuals drove it within the mentoring group, which encouraged a peer-learning environment. This learning environment creates a powerful combination of focus on individual needs, with support from co-learners that can lead to mutually beneficial and lasting results.

Peer mentoring can be highly influential; however, it needs to be set up sensitively so that there is acceptance by all parties and the understanding that it is possible to learn with and from each other. In my conclusion, peer mentoring is a dynamic form of mentoring that builds on the psychological fact that people often pay more attention to their peers' feedback, guidance, and behaviour than those in authority positions.

I have included a few templates, additional research, case studies and exercises in the following section of the workbook. I hope you find these additions of support to your practical development and understanding of the mentoring role.

Reflective log - Outtake from a trainee mentor (the peer-to-peer mentoring in Hertfordshire)

What did I do?	Started 'Looking Forward' personal/professional development group at GPT; began with an introduction to Coaching and Mentoring; flipchart work-shopping with team feedback, examining the meaning coaching, mentoring, developing an understanding, what they mean to people, how they could be applied, and what people could gain from them. We touched on practical elements such as Goal setting, which we will return to soon.
What was the effect of my actions/? behaviour?	Session received very positively; clients who are often despondent about any sort of positive future responded well to the concept of empowering change, though for some people this is a very new and scary idea. However, I definitely caught people's interest, and everyone was happy and generally enthusiastic about explore coaching and mentoring avenues further. Several people spoke to me afterwards, asking questions and taking an interest in developing further insight into these fields.
How did I feel?	This was a very good outcome which bears out my feeling that if people are given the opportunity and the tools to help themselves a good number will make the most of such opportunities. I love working with people, and it is especially gratifying to work with disadvantaged people who have a strong desire to change their circumstances for the better, so today's introductory session and its positive reception made me feel great.
What could I have done differently?	Possibly pace session a little slower to allow for more notetaking, questions etc.
What did other people think about what I did?	Client reaction was very positive, people expressing optimistic and constructive feedback. From the business point of view this is in line with business outcome requirements and fits with my remit of introducing a coaching culture, at all levels if possible, to the workplace; management feedback positive. Co-workers who support individual clients very happy with initial work.
What will I do differently?	Allow for more flexibility in session plan.
What have I learned about myself & others? What knowledge/ skills/ Insights have I gained?	This was a great opportunity to employ my presentation skills on a subject in which I believe strongly to a large group of people. The clients that I am working with have in many cases been in a relative Comfort Zone for some time, with much responsibility for their life and well-being in the care of other professionals; the concept of Change and on-going Personal Development is new to a lot of the people in the group, with some being sceptical and low on optimism.

However, I was very pleased to find that much of what we discussed was at least accepted in theory, with a good number of people becoming enthusiastic about enabling transformation. This in turn generated interest in even the most embedded individuals who conceded at least some ground, accepting at least the possibility that things could become better with a structured coaching or mentoring approach.

On the whole I was delighted by the response from the participants and although coaching and mentoring will only be one of several components of this project, I already see it as an exciting and vital set of tools in guiding people to empower their lives. |

Form 1 - Intake and completion template

Name of Mentor:
Client Reference: or name:
Start Date of Activity:
Total number of hours agreed or completed:
Upon completion of the mentoring activity: Signature of Mentor: _____ Date: _____   Signature of Mentee: _____ Date_____

Form 2 - First meeting checklist template

First meeting checklist – supporting template for mentoring sessions.

The first meeting in any mentoring relationship is vital as this is where the mentor and mentee set the frame of how the relationship will work and decide on the aims and outcomes to be accomplished.

The main objective of the initial meeting is to create a contract that will support the development of the mentoring relationship and how it will function. You should consider the following points:
- Agree boundaries and ground rules
- Establish commitment and a realistic timeline
- Explore how the relationship will develop
- Establish trust and openness
- Develop rapport by being honest with each other
- Agree common purpose and direction
- Agree how to proceed with the mentoring relationship

Pre-meeting preparation check list

- Think about your own aims and objectives in becoming a mentor
- Consider the questions your mentee might want to ask you
- Think about the first meeting and what you will need in order to make the meeting successful
- Consider how much time you and the mentee will need for this meeting and agree a date, time and place.
- Collect the relevant information from your mentee prior to the mentoring session so that you can focus on the development of the relationship.
- Think about your preferred learning style and ask the mentee about theirs, if they do not know then this could be an action for later on in the relationship.

Form 3 – Grow template

Stage	Questions	Notes
Goals Establish what the mentee wants to achieve	e.g., What would you like to get out of this mentoring session?	
Reality Consider mentee's objective in the context of the real world	e.g. What challenges or obstacles do you expect to encounter?	
Options Identify and explore different ways in which the mentee might achieve their objectives	e.g. How could you improve this situation?	
Will/Way forward Identify action points and gain commitment from the mentee	e.g. How will you feel when you achieve your goal?	

Form 4 - Case study template

Case study mentoring - This can help you to record the notes from your mentoring sessions and put forward a case study if needed.
Name:
Venue:
Confidentiality and paperwork:
Areas of discussions:
Goals and way forward:
Agreed goals:
Issues raised for next session:
Date and time of next session:

Form 5 - Personal development plan (PDP) template

This should be completed by you in the first instance and is a good tool to offer mentees, as mentoring is all about interpersonal development.

From	
To	

Planning	Professional/Personal
Your aims for working with me as a mentor. What would you like to achieve in the next 12-month period? How would you like to develop yourself? What skills will you need for the future? Are there any problems you would like to solve?	
Learning needs. What areas do you wish to develop in the next 12 months?	
Work skills. What technical skills do you need to improve in the next 12 months?	
Future Learning Needs. Where would you like to be in 3 to 5 years' time	

Form 6 - Activity planner template

	Your priorities (learning & skills needs)	How will you do this?	What help and resources do you need?	When do you hope to do this by?	When was this achieved?
1.					
2.					
3.					
4.					
5.					
6.					

Form 7 - Grid of life template

Sometimes we find ourselves struggling through life, and we have no idea why. This may be because our 'Grid of Life' has become unbalanced. This exercise is designed to look at the balance in your life and help you and your mentor identify which areas need work.

Take some time to think about your life and where you are at the present moment. Now rank your level of satisfaction with each area mentioned below by indicating which number, on a scale of 1 to 8, most closely matches how satisfied you are with that area of your life. For example, if you feel fit and well and very healthy, you might like to score your health at 7 or 8, but if you are not feeling fit and well or very healthy, you might want to score it at 3 or 4.

1. Your environment	1	2	3	4	5	6	7	8
2. Career	1	2	3	4	5	6	7	8
3. Money	1	2	3	4	5	6	7	8
4. Health	1	2	3	4	5	6	7	8
5. Friends and family	1	2	3	4	5	6	7	8
6. Significant other	1	2	3	4	5	6	7	8
7. Personal development	1	2	3	4	5	6	7	8
8. Fun and recreation	1	2	3	4	5	6	7	8

Form 7a – Grid of life template

At some time, we have all had to struggle with our life/work balance and, by being "AWARE" of what is not quite right, we can start to focus on how to move things forward. Take some time to think about how you scored yourself in the previous exercise and make notes here on how you would like things to develop.
Your environment:
Career:
Money:
Health:
Friends and family:
Significant other:
Personal development:
Fun and creativity:

Form 8 – Agreeing goals template

Agree goals in the mentoring sessions
You should prepare a detailed plan for at least one of your mentoring sessions containing enough detail for the mentee to achieve a goal or goals. The plan should be presented as part of your diary. You should work with your mentee to identify and agree on appropriate and fully SMART goals, which can cover two or more mentoring sessions. Goal setting is an essential skill that everyone needs to have. However, few people take the time to think about their goals for the short term, never mind the future. Documented information informs us that people who make goals love their lives and find more happiness, tremendous success, fulfilment, and joy. **Clarity is critical** Developing absolute clarity around what you want in life is crucial. Successful people know what they want from the future. They can create an intensity of focus that propels them towards their goals because they have such clarity. This exercise will help you plan and set goals for your mentee ensuring you stick to the SMART process.   **Specific, Measurable, Achievable, Realistic and Timed**   **GOAL ONE:**   **GOAL TWO:**

Form 9 – Reflective exercise template

Reflective Exercise
To reinforce the value of reflection, complete this short exercise by thinking of a real situation which you have experienced recently from which there has been some useful learning:

What did I do?	
How did I feel at the time?	
What was the impact or effect of my actions and behaviour?	
What could I have done differently?	
What did other people think about what I did?	
What will I do differently?	
What have I learnt about myself and others?	

Form 10 - Mentees SWOT template
A personal SWOT analysis can help you and the mentee to recognise areas of strengths and weaknesses and can be a potential focus for the mentoring relationship. The SWOT may also feed into the choice of tools and techniques you will use throughout the mentoring relationship.

The SWOT provides an overall view of the most important factors influencing the mentee's future when used correctly. The analysis is the foundation for a reflective self-assessment of how your mentee is currently performing and helps review available opportunities, reducing the fear of making the wrong decision.

Strengths	Weaknesses/Needs
Opportunities	**Barriers/Threats**

Form 11 – Supervision template

Supervision meeting with your line manager or tutor. This exercise will help you to prepare a plan for a mentoring supervision session by reviewing the mentoring activities and meetings. The exercise is only designed to give you some indicators of what you need to consider when planning the meeting.	
What did I do in order to plan the sessions?	<ul><li>I contacted my mentee by phone to outline how we were going to work.</li><li>I prepared for the meeting by putting together a mentoring pack.</li><li>I prepared some objectives for the outcomes of the session as I wanted to end the session by concluding the overall mentoring session to include agreed actions with the action plan signed.</li></ul>
Identify and agree goals with the mentee.	<ul><li>I outlined what the primary goals are. We broke the goals down by using the SMART objectives.</li><li>We put in place a timeline, with the flexibility for changes to take place, using the SMART objectives for the action plan.</li></ul>
Use questioning and listening techniques to support the mentoring role.	<ul><li>Open and closed questions were used as demonstrated in the mentoring log and case study.</li><li>Active listening was used throughout the session using body language to ensure encouraging support was offered.</li><li>Reflective practice was used by asking clarifying questions, listening and reflecting back to the mentee what was said, in order to fully check and reinforce that I was giving my full attention to the mentee, as this is a key listening skill.</li></ul>
Give feedback to the mentee to support their development	<ul><li>Use of the sandwich technique enabled me to give praise and highlight areas for personal development.</li><li>This helped the mentee to see the bigger picture of how they could implement their personal development.</li><li>The outcome for the mentee was for them to consider returning to learning by undertaking a new course in team leadership.</li></ul>
Use behaviours to develop trust	<ul><li>Agreed the notes from the session with the mentee and arranged for the mentee to have a copy of all notes.</li></ul>
What will I do differently?	<ul><li>By reviewing and summarizing my mentoring practice I am hoping that this will give me the opportunity to develop a reflective practice and gain new insights into how I have worked with the mentee, i.e.</li><li>I could have given the mentee more time for the session - at the beginning I did a lot of talking and next time I will pace myself.</li></ul>
Meeting session plan	<ul><li>The overall aim of the supervision is to enable me to have a clear frame to work with by reviewing what went well, where I can improve, and if there are any areas for concern regarding my practice or assignments.</li></ul>

Form 12 – Supervision discussion template

Coordinator/Supervisor form continued
Date

Review of supervision and areas for discussion (use the key areas below to support the review and use the review forms from your sessions with your mentee).

This will support the mentoring review, personal professional development and meet the assignment criteria. Add additional comments, notes or feedback. The rating 0 being no understanding and 5 being a high level of understanding!

Understanding	0	1	2	3	4	5	Notes
Confidence							
Knowledge							
Relationships							
Skills							
Clear objectives							
Progress towards goals							
Wellbeing							

References

Hutchinson and Hale Insights coaching and mentoring p 12 1.3 The overlap of coaching and mentoring 2012

The European and Mentoring Coaching Council (EMCC) say on their website (https://www.emccuk.org) p28 2.2

The Coaching/Mentoring Network expresses website (http://new.coachingnetwork.org.uk) p28

Sir John Whitmore/Tim Gallwey- GROW Model https://www.performanceconsultants.com/grow-model p28

Peter Hawkins Clear Model https://www.personal-coaching-information.com/clear-coaching-model.html p29

World of work the CEDAR feedback model https://worldofwork.io/2019/07/the-cedar-feedback-model/ p29

Hutchinson and Hale the INSIGHT Coaching & Mentoring Cycle developed by Eileen Hutchinson p31

Bob Bates and James McGrath. The Little Big Book of Management Theories by How to use it – Reference "The Little Big Book of Coaching Models" Published by PERSONS (my model is on page 132 model 44). p33

Eileen Hutchinson How to use the 5 E's cycle www.eileenhutchinson.com p35

Article by Sue Cullimore and Jonathan Simmons, University of the West of England, Bristol. p35

World of work Feedback Matrix https://worldofwork.io/2019/07/feedback-review-matrix/ p40

Relationships and trust (Kutilek & Earnest, 2001; Mincemoyer & Thomson, 1998). p42

Johnson (2002) www.researchgate.net/publication/232553627 p 47

APECS, the ICF, The Association for Coaching, the EMCC, CIPD and ILM page 48

EMCC Supervision Competence Framework. EMCC p49

Penny Tompkins/James Lawley "Symbolic Modelling" Metaphors in Mind 2000 p50

The Psychology of mentoring and learning by Ho Law, Sara Ireland, et al. 2007 p52

The Hutchinson's series continues with three additional workbooks

Workbook 2 "Developing Effective Coaching Skills is a 70-page workbook that provides practical tools backed up by research and theory to support the coach's role when working with team members who need to develop an awareness of capabilities, development needs, and potential. Effective Coaching links ILM level 3, 5 and 7 accreditations aimed at middle to senior managers, or freelance coaches.

This workbook will enable you to:
- Understand the significant role and responsibilities of a senior coach or mentor.
- Assess your own skills, behaviours and knowledge as a coach or mentor.
- Plan and implement further personal development via a comprehensive CPD programme.
- Plan deliver and review coaching and mentoring in an organisation or your own business.
- Expand knowledge and understanding or how coaching and mentoring can impact on people within an organisation.

Workbook 3 "Life Coaching What Really Works" – links to ILM Endorsed programme. Develop your interpersonal abilities by reading through all the essential skills, tool's techniques and requirements it takes to become an effective life or personal coach. This 70-page workbook is for anyone seeking to gain the knowledge and confidence to offer life or individual coaching. You will find this workbook to be an ideal starting point for developing a career in coaching.

This workbook will enable you to:
- Learn about life and personal coaching as a powerful development tool.
- Understand the role and responsibilities of an effective life/personal coach.
- Explore life coaching as a means of generating personal and professional change.
- Develop practical skills and learn how to set-up a coaching practice.
- Analyse, assess and plan improvements in your life while developing a coaching attitude.

Workbook 4 "Executive Coaching and Mentoring" - links to ILM level 7."
Developing executive coaching and mentoring skills ILM level 7 is for senior managers, Human Resources, HR, Organisation Development professional who wish to develop their expertise and credibility in the fields of Executive or Senior level coaching and mentoring. This 70-page workbook guides you towards becoming an Executive or Senior coach or mentor. The book is also aimed at anyone who wants to become a freelance specialist consultant.

This workbook will enable you to:
- Understand the strategic purposes of coaching and mentoring at an executive or senior level
- Analyse the knowledge, skills, behaviours and practices necessary for effective coaching or mentoring at an executive or senior level.
- Plan, deliver and review own effective coaching or mentoring at an executive or senior level.
- Learn why reflective learning is important for own professional practice.
- Be able to plan own future professional development activities as a coach or mentor operating at an executive or senior level.

Further training or consultancy in Coaching, Mentoring, Management or Leadership.
You may be interested in developing others to be coaches and mentors in the workplace, if so, we run ILM level 3, 5 or 7 coaching and mentoring certified courses.
Email info@eileenhutchinson.com www.eileenhutchinson.com
Email info@ehcoachingacademy.com www.ehcoachingacademy.com

www.ingramcontent.com/pod-product-compliance
Lightning Source LLC
Chambersburg PA
CBHW041545220526
45473CB00014B/2961